·RUDY NARAYAN·
BARRISTER FOR THE DEFENCE

TRIAL BY JURY AND HOW TO SURVIVE IT!

Barrister for the Defence

© 1985 – Rudy Narayan

Published by Justice Books, London, Justice House, 67/69 Chancery Lane, London WC2. Tel: 01-405 2105/6

Typeset by Hansib Publishing Ltd.
Cover Design: Carlton Studios
Distributed in the U.K. by:
Hansib Publishing Ltd,
Tower House,
139/149 Fonthill Road,
London, N4 3HF
Tel: 01-263 8537/8538

Dedication

To those I have drawn courage and strength from in my times of adversity: Mahatma Gandhi, Martin Luther King, Indira Gandhi, Fidel Castro, Che Guevara, Yasser Arafat, Julius Nyerere, Robert Mugabe, Jesse Jackson, Muhammad Ali, Bobby Sands and Martin McGuinness (all advocates of the ordinary man beyond compare), to Nelson Mandela (with a wonderful love), to Dean Wiley Branton and Prof. Julius Chambers (NAACP's LADF, New York), from whom I learnt much, to Mrs. Coretta King, and to the people of Brixton, London.

Acknowledgements

To Arif Ali, Kashif Ali, Jo Hall, Emerson Brathwaite for help in preparing this book; to Courtney Laws (Brixton) for my early education, to George Berry (Brixton) for completing it(!), to Rhoden Gordon (Metro 4), Brother Herman (Cricklewood 12), Cecil Gutzmore (BPIC), 'Charlie' White (Cardiff), Berry Edwards (Manchester), and James Hunte (Birmingham), for teaching me more than I can acknowledge; for Paul Boateng and Sibghat Kadri for services rendered (1980), to Donat Gomez, Franklyn Rapier, Christopher Foster and Lionel Webb among celebrated defendants, to Tony Benn (for 1980), to Paul Stephenson and Alex Pascall for friendship in adversity, to Eric Crowther QC and Tony Buck QC (for pupillage), to Zac Harazi, Cliff Lynch, Joe Hunte (dec'd), Russell Pierre, Marcus Lipton (dec'd), Clem Byfield, David Offenbach, Lord Gifford (for the early days), to Judges Gillis (retired), Miskin QC, Argyle QC, Hazan QC, The Hon. Mr. Justices Tudor, Price, Leonard, Waterhouse, Farquharson, Stocker, Peter Pain (among others, for kindness and courtesies at different times), to George Shindler QC (as he then was), the meticulous personification of professional excellence, to Lord Leslie Scarman, whose easy genius, courtesy, precision, lucidity and charm, educated me more swiftly and totally than any other person in the entire legal profession, to my "Ex" Naseem without whose help I would never have passed my Bar exams! To my friends Ashe Karim, Bob Laxman and Tom Kharran, to my dearest darling daughters and to the grassroots – may I never break the faith – One Love!

With Love!

I love the English Bar and honour many of its values and traditions. This book is written not so much in search of fault with an honourable profession but more in search of improved standards in an important area of public interest.

With all its minor blemishes and imperfections the Bar of England, subject only to a history of racial discrimination, is of high standing indeed.

Author's Note

Although real cases have been mentioned, the names of the defendants have been changed.

Contents

Minorities and the Law

Sometimes one has to play Devil's Advocate to make the point. Sometimes one has to be Critical in order to Praise.

It must never be thought that I have anything but the highest regard for the institutions mentioned herein. But to say that is not to derogate from one's highest and greater duty as a citizen to 'Speak One's Mind' in the Public Interest as opposed to the narrower, temporary self-interest of a small profession.

For too long the Bar has been, like the political parties, dominated by those who are Male, White and Middle Class, although things are now changing for the better – this book is an attempt to make the Public more aware and to make the profession more democratic, more accountable, more open to criticism and improvement and more conscious of the needs of the black, the Irish, the gay, the gypsy, the working-classes – sometimes a number of minorities can make up a majority who cannot be ignored. Indeed, outside London's Central Criminal Court, the Old Bailey, below the statue of Justice, are carved these words: "Defend the Children of the Poor and Punish the Wrongdoer."

In my experience of the criminal courts internationally the Children of the Poor, the Black and Minorities do not always start off first in the priorities of those charged with defence work (not just in England but Internationally) and this book is intended to sound the call towards heightening the Awareness and Conscience of all concerned to the crucial importance of ensuring the quality of defence work in the Criminal Courts – the blacks in Miami rioted against such courtroom injustice recently and the blacks in Brixton rioted against police injustice – the defenders must always ally themselves to Justice regardless of class, race, sex, colour or religion – the moment the defenders take sides or show prejudice is the moment when the slide from Observance and Respect to Defiance and Disrespect begins – the test of a civilised society is how it treats its minorities and the Criminal Courts often provide that acid test.

Rudy Narayan, 67 Chancery Lane, London, May 1985

Author's Introduction

This book is not so much intended to be critical of the standards of advocacy at the English Bar as to seek to improve the quality of advocacy in the criminal courts. The area of defence work is particularly crucial to the ordinary man and it is to this area that this book is directed.

While one cannot say that there are not very many excellent defence advocates at the criminal bar there is clearly room for a good many more; *it is not without significance that this is the first book ever published in the United Kingdom on defence advocacy because it has, in my view, never attracted the proper kind of professional interest.*

The comments above apply, in the broader sense, to the ranks of Queen's Counsel, too, in that they are marked more by restraint than by impetuosity and that is a criticism although they will not think it so. While the ranks of Queen's Counsel possess very many of eminence and integrity and distinction one longs for the Queen's Counsel like Michael West QC who specialises in the robust, vigorous and irresistible form of jury advocacy and the youngeer 'silks' are beginning happily to reflect some of these volatile and vibrant qualities. Come back (Judge) George Shindler QC, you are greatly missed!

What is required, of junior barrister and Queen's Counsel alike, is intellectual ability, sheer fluency in argument, a quick, clear perception and a ruthless ability to cross-examine and sum up the case with power and high persuasion. Public scrutiny of some barristers will reveal a marked social hesitation for some categories of clients, particularly Rastas, gays, gypsies, the Irish, the like.

On the other hand, names like Roy Amlot, George Carman, Jeremy Hutchinson (now Lord), Robin Simpson, Richard Du Cann, George Shindler (now Judge), Peter Pain (now a High Court Judge), Birmingham's Brian Escott-Cox and Tony Palmer, and a good many others are bywords and passwords for integrity, high competence and legendary charm, and it is a high pleasure to so record.

I mention the distinguished names above because they underline what I view to be the role of the criminal courts in a civilised society; linked invariably as it is with broken families, before and after trial, unemployment, maladjustment, racism, fascism, even naked lust and greed, it remains without doubt the most sensitive and sensational area of human activity there is and I would maintain that watching some of the above-named in action demonstrates that there is no nobler calling, no more gallant fight than that which the truly competent barrister can wage on behalf of the citizen client.

The Defence Barrister is of course barrister, father, uncle, psychiatrist, friend and brother to the man awaiting trial behind prison bars and when the criminal trial begins that ultimate trust that the prisoner reposes in him, the trust that might mean liberty or custody, must never be betrayed. Regrettably, the Bar of England is sometimes, not too often, guilty of such unintended betrayal by sending untrained men and women around the courts – when this happens (it may be the blame should be equally shared between Heads of Chambers and the School of Law) it is to be deplored, in the public interest.

This book is also necessary because it is totally vital to state clearly the case for a more dynamic and committed approach to defence work in the criminal courts. The criminal trial is no place for incompetence, inability to speak the language with precision, lucidity and eloquence (of which quite a few lawyers are guilty), or too exaggerated rituals of subservience to the Judiciary; the desire to promote one's own ambitions at the Bar, and to keep "in" with the profession, sometimes dictates a lack of total commitment of some defenders. The Judiciary, too, is not without some, happily only a few, members whose racism and class-prejudice, having survived their promotion, continues to dictate sometimes foolish and overtly prosecution-oriented conduct of the criminal trial. But this handful, rapidly diminishing, are the rare exceptions, not the rule. On the other hand the citizen appearing before distinguished tribunals like Mr. Justice Skinner, Mr. Justice Pain, Mr. Justice Waterhouse, Mr. Justice Farquharson, Mr Justice McCowan, among others, finds himself dazzled by courtesy, correctness, kindness and pre-eminent distinction. A top English High Court Judge in full cry is a treat to see and a professional experience of rarity and vintage and Lord Scarman remains the most dazzling example of all.

The object of Counsel for the Defence should be to test with the Burning Sword approach all evidence placed before him with a total and dynamic application; some defences, like the trial of Rasta youth Christopher Smith, require the sending of an armada of burning ships among the bulwarks of the often-leaking vessels of the prosecution fleet whose powder is not always dry; and one or two defences, as with some Rastas who claim police perjury, will require Counsel to stand up to the trial judge in sheer fighting determination and ensure acquittal of the innocent client who is sometimes being framed by corrupt police. Contrary to popular legend, the brighter and more able your trial judge, the greater graciousness and respect he will accord the tenacious Defence Counsel – as long as you yourself are respectful and able. More than 98 per cent of criminal cases involve the working-class defendant.

Still too many Defence Counsel are not knowledgeable enough about the background of their clients and the sociological reasons for their "crimes". One would almost argue for sociology to be a compulsory subject for a would-be Defence Barrister!

A number of defence barristers, black and white, are incompetent and would not be allowed to practise by the standards of other professions like medicine or accountancy. Some barristers for the defence, too many, are guided by the instinct of self-preservation against tough Judges and so find the will to fight diluted and eroded.

The public provides the purse that pays largely for the services of defence barristers. The public should exercise a continual vigilance to ensure the continuing high quality in what it pays for.

This book calls for a most thorough and public debate on the quality of defence work afforded the public by the British legal profession so that the public interest and public debate takes permanent priority. While ranking the personal integrity of the English Bar as second-to-none, there is clear room for improvement on matters of courtroom competence.

The criminal courts can ensure the liberty of the subject or the loss of it. It is a crucial area. The public deserves the best. Integrity is there, competence needs constant attention.

It is high time that he who pays the piper calls the tune. The legal profession would gain much by being more open and accountable to public scrutiny.

It is my hope that youngsters aspiring to the Bar will consider lending their talents to the defence as opposed to the prosecution and that those presently going through the schools of law will ensure over the next decade what we do not yet have – a clearly identifiable cadre of fighting barristers specialising only in defence work. I have tried to set out in this book, with illustrations from actual cases, the lessons of sixteen gladatorial and sometimes incandescent years and the best thing I could wish for a young barrister is that he grows up to be a defender trusted by the citizen client; after all, the sweetest and most eloquent sound to the defendant's ears are those two little words from the foreman of the jury – "Not Guilty".

Rudy Narayan, Justice House, 67/69 Chancery Lane, London, WC2. May 1985.

Prologue

"Not Guilty, Rastafari!"

Watching BBC Television Breakfast Time news on the morning of Thursday, 23rd August, 1984, I saw scenes of South African policemen attacking the heads of black demonstrators with their truncheons with a vicious savagery; the blacks had been impertinent enough to protest against South Africa's "liberal" electoral system which allowed Asians and "Coloureds" places in Parliament but excluded the Africans; but it was the scenes of arrogant savagery which suddenly banished the sleep from my eyes and made me sit up. The first policeman to chase one particular black demonstrator was aiming his baton clearly and coolly for the man's head and he hit him at least four times the head, yet the black kept on running; when that particular policeman tired of his sport the poor black probably thought the chase was over as he straightened himself up, only to see another vicious policeman come swinging in, again for the head, with crunching blows. And this little bit of newsreel encapsulates, for me, the rejection with which some in the British police, lawyers, media, magistracy and judiciary view the Rastafarian in British Society – indeed, the South African policemen's savagery was exceeded only by an attack on Brixton's Lloyd Coxsone that I once witnessed in Brixton's Railton Road (on a day after the Brixton riots) where a Brixton officer simply ran amok with a truncheon at Coxsone's head; it is something of a reflection of the magical quality of the spirituality of the Rasta that Lloyd Coxsone lived to forgive his abusers by playing cricket with them where others could have rushed to seek revenge. But the above illustrates a particular problem of a section of British society who are too often and too much and too openly despised by some of those in authority and offer sad prey to the racists among some police and some tribunals alike who tremble at the sight of the glorious locks of the Sons of Zion which, instead of awakening an appreciative spirituality, sometimes awakens a nasty hostile reaction. (Not so, with Judge Argyle!)

The trial of Rasta Christopher Smith illustrates the viciousness that Rastas still meet and it is worthy of separate record in this book.

Christopher Smith was a tall, proud youth who lived in South London. In April, 1983, Smith was charged with a total of twelve armed robberies by

Catford Police. He was indicted before an Old Bailey jury and the prosecution case rested largely on what the prosecution alleged were 'voluntary' confessions signed by Smith. Defence Barrister Edmond Alexander led for the Defence. The Defence alleged that Smith had been a critic of South London police and had spoken on platforms over the Deptford Fire case. Further, Smith alleged at his trial that he had been the victim of much violence by the officers concerned. If the police had truly been violent to him before extracting "confessions" then the confessions could not possibly be treated as "voluntary" and the jury would be entitled, nay duty-bound, to throw the confessions out and acquit Smith. The jury found Christopher Smith "Not Guilty!" of each and every charge against him and the Rasta walked free, but more was to come.

Some six months later Smith was again arrested by South London police, this time once on a charge of murder and once more found himself before an Old Bailey jury. His first trial took place before His Honour Judge Tudor Price QC, the Common Sergeant of London (now a High Court Judge), always a model of courtesy and correctness. Kenneth Richardson QC, one of Britain's top prosecutors, appeared for the Crown. The eternal Edmond Alexander appeared for Smith (led by a legendary Guyanese barrister who has to be nameless!), Richard Du Cann QC, another figure of legal legend, appeared for one of Smith's co-defendants and Patrick Back QC, the very personification of 'Silk', appeared for another. It was going to be a hard trial. The prosecution witnesses took to the witness box.

The police case against Smith and his co-defendants began in a jewellery shop in Greenwich where a member of the shop sadly met her death during a robbery by three blacks which went wrong. Smith's two co-defendants had made statements to the police in which they admitted their part in the robbery but stated that it was Smith who had a knife, that Smith was the man who struck the fatal blow and that the two of them were totally unaware of the presence of a knife. They both admitted the crime of robbery but pleaded "Not Guilty!" to murder. These two co-defendants were to stick to their guns and accuse Smith in similar terms in the first trial (Smith was re-tried later). But when they gave evidence it was pointed out in cross-examination by Smith's Counsel that they had given the police versions which contradicted that which they gave the Old Bailey jury (and so their evidence did not achieve anything of that high quality which the prosecution required.)

Turning away from the evidence of the co-defendants, the police pointed out that Smith had been identified at the police station by at least two members of the public, one being a member of the shop. But, as the defence pointed out, the method of identification employed was something bizarre. Smith was held by his locks "like a wounded animal" while he bled onto the floor of the police room police staged "a confrontation" with witnesses!

Without waiting for his solicitor, Mr Ashe Karim, who was then speeding his way across London to the police station, "they were so propelled by indecent haste" said Defence Counsel, and "so callously lacking in any kind of humanity for this injured man that they could not even stop to get him medical attention for his bleeding injuries" – they held him roughly by his locks and so, according to Defence Counsel, "engineered what they are now pleased to call evidence of identification." But there was more to come upon the question of identification.

The police had made up a photofit picture of the "tall" man – the man the Prosecution said was Smith although, as the Defence pointed out to the Old Bailey jury, "this picture does not look at bit like Christopher Smith!" Further, it transpired that a Security Guard had recognised the "tall" man on the very day of the robbery/murder but the Prosecution did not call this witness and the reason was made clear by the Defence. For when this vital witness looked at Smith in the police station he told police: "Definitely not him!" This evidence was called by the Defence (but made available by the Prosecution.)

Aha, shouted the Prosecution, all is not yet over – "when Smith was in police custody he jumped through a first floor window!" "Why," asked the Prosecution in sepulchral tones, "does a man jump out of windows of a police station unless he is guilty of that with which he is accused?" But, although the police clutched at this particular straw the jury did not jump because, as the Defence pointed out, "if you had once nearly had your brains beaten out by officers who had then tried to frame you for crimes you had not committed" (a reference to Smith's previous acquittal), "and now were again confronted by police officers seemingly bent on framing you for murder, you might jump through the windows of a police station not once but three times!"

The first Old Bailey jury, torn between the conflicts of evidence could, not agree after a long day's retirement and Smith was sent for re-trial. (His two co-defendants were both convicted of manslaughter.)

When the re-trial came it came before the Recorder of London, a judge who has a reputation among some Defence Lawyers as a judge who does not take lightly to defendants launching irresponsible attacks on the police but nevertheless a judge who plays with a Clive Lloyd straight bat strictly down the line and; this difficult trial was to prove to be no exception to the distinguished talents of this eminent judge.

At the second trial the two co-defendants, having themselves been convicted, now appeared simply as Prosecution witnesses. But this time round they stated that Smith was not the "tall" man and they gave the name of the other man. Faced with this withdrawal, once again the Defence mounted a vigorous onslaught on the way in which the police had treated Smith at the police station. "They treated this man with total arrogance and contempt and it is a matter for you, members of the jury, how you treat this kind of shabby identification obtained in this brutal and callous way."

The second jury still could not agree and the Prosecution took the hint and called it a day. Smith walked free from the Old Bailey for the second time in one year and this itself is a record. But the lessons of this case are wider and more far-reaching.

When a rich man or an influential man like, say, Jeremy Thorpe, is arrested he is attended immediately by his lawyers and arrested by appointment! The rich and the powerful have this immense advantage. But the poor man, the black man, especially the Rasta, too often has his civil rights trampled upon by police. Added to this, while the rich man can pick and choose his lawyer and hire and fire at his will (or purse!) the poor man is sometimes saddled with some very unfortunate Legal Aid bedfellows which he cannot get rid of without bowing and scraping to some hostile stipendiary magistrate. Legal Aid Certificates are the manacles and chains of the poor and the black and there is a growing menace to the human rights of poor defendants in that the authorities, once a man is chained to the Duty Solicitor or to the first solicitor on the scene, do not easily allow him in time freedom of choice of lawyers. This contempt is nearly always highlighted with the Rasta defendant in the English courts.

Further, the way in which South London police allegedly treated Christopher Smith is an experience a lot of Rastas go through and which few Defence Barristers can successfully attack at trial. Police at the highest levels should ensure that no section of society, no matter how small, powerless, unpopular or vulnerable can make this allegation – since the ultimate test of a civilised society is how it treats its minorities.

Further, Rastas appearing in the Old Bailey dock are not always accorded the same respect and courtesy by some members of the Judiciary and it takes a Barrister of some strong nerve to ensure that both Justice and Courtesy attend his Rasta client. But witness the care, concern and sympathy of Judge Argyle QC!

Further, some of the ushers and the clerks and the court officers (happily only a few) of the British courts are known to snigger and smirk too often when a Rasta gives evidence which is accusatory of police. And some few judges find it difficult to maintain their customary balance when such attack comes from such an unconventional source.

Finally, Fleet Street is always on the hunt for stories of Rastas convicted of crimes so that if middle-class Englishmen and poverty-stricken Rasta commit the same crime then somehow the crime becomes greater and more sensational if the defendant is Rasta.

The Rasta may smoke their weed and "do their thing" but the "true Rasta" is basically the most spiritual and gentle of people – and police, media, lawyers and Judiciary have a worrying record to wipe out in their treatment of defendants like Christopher Smith who may have to walk long walks and climb tall mountains before hearing those sweet words from a jury: "Not Guilty, Rastafari!"

Part I

CHAPTER ONE

Role and Function of Counsel for the Defence

The role and function of Counsel for the Defence is not in any way to attempt to deceive a jury in coming to the wrong conclusion. The duty of Defence Counsel is to point out to a jury signposts along the way of evidence which will assist the jury in coming to a proper and fair conclusion "upon the evidence", for the oath the jury takes is to come to a verdict upon the evidence and not upon conjecture and speculation.

A proper and fair conclusion may be Guilty or Not Guilty, it matters not which, as long as the verdict is totally consistent with the evidence.

Counsel for the Defence stands between the court and the defendant as the total and supreme filter – no evidence that is false, unreliable, unfair or prejudicial must pass his eagle eye and sharp talons; Counsel for the Defence is the Burning Sword that purges lying witnesses, unreliable memories and prejudicial or unfair evidence or interference that the prosecution through ineptness or a judge through incompetence or bias might otherwise let through to a jury.

The minds of the jury are of course Holy Ground and every criminal trial is, in a way, a battle of persuasion, honest persuasion on the evidence, for the hearts and minds of that random group of twelve ordinary citizens sworn as judges of the facts. An advocate blessed with careful preparation, swift perception, speech in cross-examination quicker than the witness's thought, wit, eloquence, humour and personality can literally build bricks from straws but he should have regard to the evidence and do so honestly and realistically.

A shrewd appreciation of how quickly and pleasantly, sometimes abrasively, to engage the collective personality of the jury is one of the finer talents of the best advocates.

Apart from the purging of unreliable evidence Counsel for the Defence must act as a medium of communication for the defendant and his witnesses.

Defendants by definition are not equipped with policemen's notebooks from which zombie-like to recite their evidence, true or false. They have to be "led" in the giving of their evidence so that the listening jury can tune in quickly and accurately to the wavelength of the defence and the personality of the defendant. It is a mistake to assume that the wavelength used by the prosecution is the very same radio frequency to be used to broadcast the message of the defence. In many cases, the defence has a vested interest in moving the pitch of its defence to VHF as opposed to the prosecution's droning Lotus-Eaters style of Medium Wave!

Before Counsel for the Defence can even begin to act as a medium of communication he must first both know his client, know his case, know the jury and watch that old judge perched up there! Some judges, like, for example, the Common Sergeant, His Honour Judge Tudor Price QC, sitting at London's Old Bailey, are bywords for courtesy and fairness but every prison grapevine is filled with rumour and gossip about judicial bias, happily not too widespread. This four-fold task of knowing client, case, jury and judge is easier to state than to achieve.

Counsel for the Defence can easily master the *facts* of his case if he really wants to by reading, re-reading and triple-reading his brief time and time again. Mere repetition with a reasonably alert mind should be enough. It is not without significance that the massively successful defenders are noted for the tremendous assiduity with which they marshall and master the facts in their briefs. But, in this regard, because of the social background (or even the pretended social background!) of some barristers they do not "get across" to their largely working-class clients. Black defendants experience much of this kind of difficulty with white barristers, with certain honourable exceptions.

Generally speaking, Counsel who has mastered his facts, knows his judge and who understands his client is at a massive advantage when addressing a jury.

The role and function of Counsel for the Defence, therefore, is to assist the court in the most severe and vigorous testing of the prosecution case consistent with his instructions, intelligent infer-ences that might properly be drawn from the evidence in the case and consistent with his duty to be honest with the court and to be realistic with the jury. Upon the question of reasonable inferences from the evidence, there is an instance recorded when His Honour Judge Abdela QC, for whom I have the highest regard, regretfully complained to the Professional Conduct Committee of the Senate about a barrister who utilised evidence coming from prosecution witnesses and adopted such evidence as his own; perfectly proper, of course, and the fact that the P.C.C. threw out the complaint emphasises this point. Counsel for the Defence should address the jury as "seekers after the Truth" within the context of the rules of procedure and evidence and, properly pursued, there is no nobler task that one man might perform for another.

For if a man be innocent or falsely charged what nobler crusade for a lawyer to embark on than the destruction in a court of law of the lies and deception of a dishonest prosecution? Here the words "dishonest prosecution" do not refer to Prosecution Counsel, although some Counsel for the Prosecution can be sometimes shown to be less than fair and Prosecution Counsel should never be automatically exempt from suspicion in sensitive and troublesome cases. In this context, recounting the Terry May Murder Trial at London's Old Bailey in 1982, both defence and jury were fortunate enough to have Counsel of impeccable integrity, Roy Amlot, leading for the Crown before a tremendous judge, Mr. Justice Farquharson.

If the evidence be unreliable then the acquittal of a defendant is both desirable and right.

Non-lawyers always ask me: "But how can barristers defend a man when you know he is Guilty?" The answer is as follows: "If a defendant *states* to his barrister he is Guilty as charged then it is the duty of Counsel for the Defence to advise him to plead Guilty or withdraw from the case."

It is dishonest to act in any other way and the Knight in Shining Armour Image much tarnished thereby. It is absolutely no part of the duty of Counsel for the Defence to prostitute himself in the scurrilous defence of a guilty and lying defendant.

But, equally, where instructions are clear and consistent upon the basis of innocence then Counsel for the Defence must brook no interference, allow no obstacle, and never stand aside from the pursuit of his client's acquittal. In the murder case of Jamaican defendant Donat Smith (See *Who Killed Maureen Armstrong?* by Rudy Narayan) the client got off but Defence Counsel got six months! If, in the pursuit of this honourable duty, Counsel meets with confrontations with police and/or judge then there is no escape – let it be confrontation as long as an innocent man is not convicted!

The role of Counsel for the Defence is a most precious role which should be jealously guarded at all times and in all places and Counsel should never allow his voice to be stifled or his stance to be shifted – "None Shall Pass" until Truth and Justice run free within the criminal courts of England; and this is a proper steed to be mounted by those who would embark on a Crusade for Truth and the Vindication of the Innocent in the courts of England.

CHAPTER TWO

Role and Function of Counsel for the Prosecution

The duty of Counsel for the Prosecution (Counsel for the "Crown" is a misnomer in the same way that in the U.S.A. *The People* versus O'Hara is accurate) is to present the evidence to the court fully, fairly and honestly; some such Counsel, very few, tend to overlook this high duty. Prosecution Counsel is under a permanent and total duty to be frank with the court and the defence at all times.

The duty of frankness with the defence, for example, includes the automatic revelation of all criminal convictions of every single prosecution witness upon whose evidence they seek to invite the jury to convict; regrettably, too many Prosecution Barristers, especially the younger ones, are too often given to severe lapses of memory on this point and need to be jogged pretty sharply in their pseudo-aristocratic ribs. Previous convictions of prosecution witnesses are always most relevant to Defence Counsel when considering, in a given case, whether attack be the best form of defence and this information, if not given freely, should be demanded. This is an area of sometimes vital information which can often be most effectively used in cross-examination. In a defence where the defendant's own previous criminal record is going to be tossed hatlike "into the ring" this information can sometimes more than balance the scales of credibility.

It is always the duty of Prosecution Counsel to make available to the defence *statements* of a prosecution witness inconsistent with or contradictory to the *evidence* of that particular witness (or indeed previous statements of the same witness which contradict each other in a manner favourable to the defence). In the now legendary murder trial of Jamaican Donat Smith (1974 for four months at Stafford Crown Court), this duty of disclosure was sadly neglected by the prosecution in that previous inconsistent statements of particular witnesses were never disclosed to the defence. Such failure to disclose need not always be taken as the product of dishonesty on the part of prosecution counsel. In an enquiry involving hundreds of statements, such as the case of Donat Smith clearly entailed, prosecution counsel can so easily fail to make himself familiar with the contents of bundles of statements marked "irrelevant" by police and prosecution authority. Strictly speaking, of course, such default lies at the door of Counsel who really should be familiar with all contradictory material within the statements.

In the case of Donat Smith the inadvertent omissions of Leo Clarke QC (as he then was) were more than remedied by his learned Junior, Christopher Oddie (now His Honour Judge Oddie), making all such bundles totally available for inspection. In the event, some rather startling aspects of the prosecution case were rectified by the nasty, suspicious mind of Junior Counsel for the Defence, one Harry Narayan, who stayed up till the early hours of the morning and who found very many statements (from witnesses not called by the prosecution!) which were consistent with the innocence of the defendant Smith. Key witnesses for the prosecution had their evidence nullified by their own previous inconsistent statements or by contradictory statements of other persons.

As an example of such omission in the case of Smith, the prosecution called evidence to show that a length of rope found in the boot of Smith's car had recent bloodstaining on it and so they invited the jury to consider whether such bloodstains might not be that of the victim. But inspection of the so-called bundle of "irrelevant" statements brought forth witnesses and evidence (known to the police!) which showed that a furniture shop salesman had helped Smith load and tie an offending settee to the roof of his car. The salesman had cut his finger on the rope leaving his blood there ... an extraordinary and dangerous omission! Other dangerous omissions in this troubled case involved evidence called by the prosecution to establish that bits of white paint found under the victim's fingernails matched the paint of Smith's car! What they forgot to place before the jury was that the dead woman's residential quarters had, just prior to her death, been repainted with just such paint and therefore that paint could have come, not just from Smith's car but also the victim's own residence! And yet this is precisely the sort of evidence which, if uncontradicted, even though the police knew of such contradictions, could have convicted an innocent man of murder.

This area therefore is well worthy of a nasty, suspicious mind and Prosecution Counsel must be asked about these matters and well in advance of trial.

Prosecution Counsel should be not only of the highest integrity but of total competence with the highest sense of professional duty. Happily, integrity is seldom ever lacking but competence is not a byword for the Prosecution List and pro-police bias is sometimes present in Counsel's row.

What is sadly lacking from the majority is that delightful alliance between integrity, fairness and competence free of police bias that make names like Michael Corkery, John Matthew, Roy Amlot, etc. glowing Jewels of The Crown. But, as I say, the majority are not of that same pinnacle of high competence. Whenever prosecution counsel is known to be unfair that reputation is nearly always allied to incompetence. Prosecution Counsel, of course, are advocates for matters brought by the police. The police are their effective "instructors" and this should be remembered.

There are substantial and regular earnings to be made for those Counsel who are found "pleasing" by the police. The temptation is nearly always there, therefore, for prosecution counsel to lean heavily in favour of the police; luckily, this temptation is seldom yielded to.

Whenever this temptation is yielded to it is indeed a sad spectacle, for Counsel should never be hostages to Fortune (or fortunes, which are there to be made from regular prosecution work.)

Prosecution Counsel are agents of the Crown, as indeed the Judiciary are. Unless they are totally incompetent (or damned fools) all that they offer to the court finds sympathetic ears. They therefore have a far easier task and have very few confrontations with judges indeed.

However, generally speaking, integrity is there and what they must be watched for is occasional police bias and the duty of full disclosure already mentioned. Because they have "friends at court" the sense of pressure that the ruthless prosecutor can exert is quite astonishing and, if it is found, ruthlessness must be met with equal firmness. Quickly find the measure of your Prosecutor and act accordingly.

While upon the subject, at a time when British courts are filling up the Borstals with 40% black inmates andprisons with 25% black inhabitants, it is extremely sad to have witnessed the racist refusal of the authorities, right up to 1984, to refuse to allow too many black barristers to prosecute, or to be appointed judges. When an all-white police force has been meting out brutality and perjury to the blacks for the last two decades it has taken white prosecutors to defend the police against defence allegations. As I write, in George Orwell's 1984, no black person has been allowed to take part in any significant prosecution ever. The last two years has seen one or two blacks allowed to prosecute but, as always, it is the Kellogg's Cornflakes blacks, who have first been most carefully vetted by the security services.

CHAPTER THREE

Holding the Scales in Equal Balance

The role of the judge in the British criminal courts should be that of umpire and referee. He should be totally courteous, impartial and stunningly honest in his conduct of trials. He must be above reproach, like Ceasar's wife before him; and, like Ceasar's wife, the judge should sometimes be a woman (or, dare I whisper it, even a black!). "All things must count with him but none too much." He should concern himself not with personalities but with the evidence. One cannot prize too highly the gloriously objective handling of the murder trial of Mohammed Khan in the Cardiff Crown Court by Mr. Justice Waterhouse in late 1983; if a transcript were offered for sale of the interventions of this judge in this case then you would find it copybook stuff. Like Mr. Justice Waterhouse and, in addition, Mr. Justice Farquharson, Mr. Justice Skinner and Mr. Justice McCowan among others, the trial judge should avoid discourtesy and should himself be a personification of justice and fair play. He should not take sides with prosecution or defence but should treat all alike with the greatest respect. Like the American judges (but sadly unlike some British ones) he should never allow his views to intrude upon the trial. I once heard the Lord Chief Justice of Alberta address a juvenile defendant brought up for cattle-rustling as "Sir"! How often do you find this in British courts? I once heard the Judge Advocate at an American court-martial simply direct his court-martial jury in this way: "You have heard the evidence. I will now read you the law. The verdict is for you." When British judges criticise their American brothers I fear that there is some hypocrisy about. American courts even allow British television cameras into their courtrooms (see Walter Merricks in "Circuit II – Miami"). British courts would never dream of allowing in microphones. *Res ipsa loquitur.*

The personification of a truly admirable judge was the former Recorder at London's Old Bailey, Sir Carl Aarvold, a judge of impeccable courtesy, kindness and objectivity, a man whose personal integrity illuminated the office he graced. Unfortunately, there are not too many like him about today. Although the coming of Lord Chief Justice Geoffrey Lane has brightened up the judicial horizon with engaging no-nonsense frankness there are still too many surly judges around and one would like to see citizen-participation in the election of judges. In the United States, judges put their entire private and professional career on public trial when they stand for election but British judges are appointed by a secret process which sometimes makes surprising appointments.

Most criminal court judges are drawn from the ranks of former Prosecution Counsel and sometimes a few openly take sides with the police. Attacks as in the murder case of Rastafarian Christopher Smith, who accused South London police of perjury and fabrication of evidence, arouse the resentment of some judges and, after telling juries that "the facts are for you", these few then embark on regrettable excursions of trying to influence the verdict of the jury by a hostile summing-up; unfortunately, the Court of the Appeal does not lightly take to judges being accused of bias or even of racism, and, once appointed, it is hard to remove biased judges; although one with bias is one too many.

Counsel for the Defence may only, of course, launch such attacks on instructions but even where the evidence is consistent with police perjury some few of Her Majesty's judiciary fail to maintain that semblance of judicial impartiality; the result is emotionally disheartening and intellectually sad. Judges should not allow their own views on the evidence to influence a jury. But from time to time, the young Counsel for the Defence will be disillusioned as some judges give their own interpretations of the evidence. They give the traditional warning of course, that the jury is entitled to reject their views, but coming from so distinguished a source, who is there to say what havoc judicial views wreak upon the considerations of many a jury? This habit of English judges to offer their own views, is, to be fair, sanctioned by the Court of Appeal and I would argue that the Court of Appeal is wrong not to come down heavily on these occasional judicial excursions into the realms of the facts, almost usurping the role of the jury. One favourite aside by certain judges is to preface all their pro-prosecution remarks with the catch-phrase "The prosecution argue that ..." when no such argument has been advanced by prosecution counsel!

The judges of England have many discretionary powers, too many in my view, but this licence to comment approved by the Court of Appeal is one that brings many sarcastic comments from overseas visitors to the public galleries. It should be a matter of public debate whether such judicial licence to comment should not be restricted to follow the more impartial conduct of the American judiciary. What price would a young Counsel for the Defence pay for a judicial summing-up limited to a simple, lucid exposition of the law and a simple balanced statement of the evidence with no hints or innuendos!

Subject to the above reservations, the judges of England are an independent breed free of fears of easy dismissal or of pressure from the Executive. Their integrity, compared internationally, is legend. But there remains the limitation that they are drawn almost exclusively from the ranks of Prosecution Counsel and this background sometimes induces not a deliberately dishonest but a pre-coloured approach to the criminal trial.

The other matter is this. Most criminal trials are, of course, born of sociological causes, as every resident Law Centre worker knows. Bad housing, family breakup, unemployment, personality disorders, etc. all play their part in the whole theatre of criminal conduct. A few judges are totally unaware of the sociological cause and content of criminal behaviour and while they pay something more than lip service to Social Enquiry Reports they tend to view sentencing, some of them, as punishment rather than reformation. What a pleasure it is when the public is treated to an enlightened judge who truly makes "the punishment fit the crime." Too little use is made of community service orders where, for example, the defendant who mugged an old lady could be sentenced to 100 hours of cleaning her back garden rather than getting bitter and twisted in Borstal. Penalties should be more aimed towards rehabilitation and less towards revenge, and young Counsel for the Defence should know this. Further, in respect of the black defendant, especially the Rasta, the gipsy, the homosexual, or the squatter, there is sometimes manifested in judicial pronouncements a lack of sympathy for the predicament of minorities, and it took Lord Scarman in his report on the Brixton Riots to place the plight of the minorities in proper judicial perspective. The statement made at the Old Bailey that "the coming of blacks to Clapham and Brixton made once-safe areas dangerous to live in" was a model of judicial stupidity in that it ran contrary to the experience of older white Brixtonians who remember muggings in the pre-war and pre-black days. Judges' utterances, especially in sentencing, have the advantage, if sensational enough, to command instant media attention, and the vultures of the gutter press are able to depend with nauseating frequency on such sensation which too often attends the sentencing of members of minorities. Judicial utterances, outside of the bare limits of the words of sentence, should avoid spreading resentment and recrimination and should be models of moderation. Remembering as I do the Lord Chief Justice of Alberta addressing his cattle-rustler with "Sir", a few judges in England should learn never to rob a defendant of his fundamental right to be called "Mr", in a way that leaves him naked and without dignity.

CHAPTER FOUR

The Weapons of the Courts

Language is of course the main weapon of the courtroom and there should be no hiding place for the practitioner who mumbles and bumbles his way through cross-examinations and through inept and unworthy speeches.

There is no excuse for lack of fluency in the legal profession and no young practitioner should dream of imposing himself on the profession without the ability to articulate swiftly, fluently and with total lucidity. Inability in public speaking is incompetence and incompetence is a form of dishonesty. The Bar has recently brought in new rules about aspiring barristers needing to have good second-class degrees before qualifying for Law School but they still do not do enough about advocacy. Prospective members of the profession should attend every single debate, visiting speaker, meeting, moot or mock trial at university because while the prepared speech will do for one's final speech to the jury, cross-examination involves quick thinking on one's feet and literally grasping the witness's answer in mid-air and turning it back on him like a swiftly resharpened knife. The young law student must learn to argue well and to debate well and must conquer any nervousness about public speaking long before beginning pupillage.

The qualities of the successful Counsel for the Defence will include a reasonably smart appearance coupled with presence and personality. Shabbily presented Counsel nearly always offer shabbily presented arguments.

But for as long as the English language remains the language of the land then for so long will its mastery be the first prerequisite of any aspiring practitioner. To this end it is my sad duty to say that the language of certain barristers is a disgrace to the profession and a further disgrace is that they make no attempt to improve on their lack of fluency. The Bar should seriously consider either disbarring or restraining those who are not fluent in the courts. For it is language that persuades juries and the enthusiastic cultivation of a free, eloquent and lucid style is not only an asset, it is a barrister's first duty. The mastery and command of language includes not only a wide vocabulary but an eloquent assembling of words with quickfire timing. Cross-examination must of absolute necessity be free-flowing and barristers must be able to place words together as with the rapid firing of a machine gun. Words, used swiftly and accurately, are like bullets and, in this context, they can kill off feeble prosecutions. Sometimes, sheer eloquence can even ward off certain conviction by splitting juries down the middle twice around and getting an acquittal where there normally would be none! Words by Counsel must be logical and must make sense to even the most illiterate juror and they must capture the mind of even the most hostile ones; nothing less than immediate call on a plenteous eloquence will suffice. If you tend to be halting and fumbling with words then take up canecutting where the only weapon you require is a cutlass, and this advice goes for some of my very best friends! To advocate eloquence is not to argue that words should not be used economically; many a witness has been caught up in the crossfire of fluent but controlled cross-examination. One of the finest examples of fluent but controlled use of language was George Shindler QC (now His Honour Judge Shindler), and many juniors and many seniors too would have gained much from emulating his style. Shindler QC was also, when he was still at the Bar, one of the finest examples of presence. Presence is easy to feel but hard to define; but one can begin by stating that the Bar is a hard taskmaster requiring physical fitness, intellectual stamina and emotional balance. It is a profession for strong men, not weaklings. Barristers need to master their papers, to quickly establish trust with their clients and then they must move on to dominate the courtroom with style and charisma. They need to face obstacles of evidence and law, the anxieties of the client and the personalities of judge and jury and begin and end a case with total control, and, convicted or acquitted, retain their unique and distinctive aplomb. Such control of events and personality approaches self-mastery and when it all combines together it establishes presence. Well-cut suits, polished manners and pleasant demeanour may add to presence but can never be a substitute for it. Presence of the positive kind can be positively intimidating and there is much to be said for beginning a case with that rare impact.

The quality of analysis of the evidence in the antiseptic quietude of Chambers must be allied to an almost instinctive perception of witnesses' psychology. Bearing in mind that a lot of police officers come up for questioning the best preparation for advocacy and cross-examination would be service in the armed forces rather than three years at university. Perception must be in a moment and must be quick, sharp and accurate. Perception comes from a knowledge of the ways of the world and an experience of life. If you cannot pack a lifetime of brothels and personal drug-addiction into three years of university then read biography about the seedy side of life! Couple it with as much contact with the poor and the deprived as you can. Work in a community project, go grassroots, lend your hand – and voice – to anything, but get experience of people in rough places enjoying rough times. Lord Denning, despite his late-in-life blunders over blacks in and out of the profession, was still probably the greatest judge of this century and always told law students to read anything but law.

When you come to the Bar you will find some mentally-tottering types and you must not be too shattered by the experience. The ranks of the Bar contain far too many decrepit and burnt-out hulks who, the captaincy of judgeships having been denied them, cling limpet-like to the profession. But they are not to be disregarded because of antiquity. Remember that competence lies not always with the seniors: you can bring your own brand and style with you to refresh the ancient cobwebs in the darkest corners of the Inner Temple.

The criminal courts are, of course, largely theatre and, although there is no justification for sheer histrionics, knowledge of audience (jury) psychology and certain limited histrionics of voice and gesture are useful. Without playing to the public gallery, the jury is still an audience and a question asked in cross-examination can register that much more impact if volume and tone of voice is right. Judges in summing-up make heavy use of inflexions and tone of voice and Counsel for the Defence has to be prepared to perceive, anticipate and match judicial psychology. Make no mistake about this, the criminal trial is a battle for the minds of the jury and prosecution counsel seeks only one verdict. Once a prosecution is begun then they seek a conviction. Every opening in the prosecution case has to be exposed, every chink in their armour revealed. Hence the origin of the saying "All is fair in Love, War and the Criminal Trial!"

Counsel for the Defence needs to be possessed of the most dynamic and enquiring mind as he sets out to test reliable evidence and to seek out, find and destroy dishonest witnesses. There is no peace for the wicked and no rest for Counsel for the Defence from beginning to end. A phrase, a word, an aside may sometimes turn the scales and all must be preparation, alertness, perception and swiftness of execution;

simplicity and lucidity make good bedfellows before a jury.

Counsel for the Defence is no good to anybody unless he is possessed of total integrity in his dealings with solicitors, client, prosecution and the court. There are certain ground rules which must be obeyed and they are all of them born of honest, open conduct. Better to appear before a Disciplinary Tribunal for being outspoken than for being dishonest.

Counsel for the Defence must see himself as a medium, a channel for the truth; it is only if an acquittal is brought about by an honest, realistic and open defence that Counsel is entitled to bask in the heady afterglow of professional conceit. There are unfortunately to my knowledge certain defence lawyers, solicitors more often than barristers, who "coach" their clients in their evidence and cross that very thin but precious line between rehearsal of true evidence and suggesting what a client's defence might be. If all instructions come wholly from the client then there is nothing wrong in going over precisely what he has told his solicitors if only to check consistency, but barristers must never ever suggest a single word of their client's defence. In this context, if your client's instructions "change" at any time between receipt of your brief and the conclusion of the trial then it is best to get your solicitors to instruct you further in writing. The date and time of the amended instructions should be noted and unless the new changes amount to a basic contradiction of your earlier instruction then, armed with written amendments, it is proper to proceed. To co-operate with a false defence knowingly is dishonest, immoral and of course a criminal offence; some barristers have behaved from time to time in this way but most of them have been disbarred: such people are the dregs of the profession since they aim to achieve by deceit what they cannot achieve by good, honest practice. While the duty of all lawyers is to fight to the last drop for the defence of a client who protests his innocence their weapons in the fight must be clear-cut honesty and, one hopes, more dynamic application to facts and law. The morality of the profession is to assist the course of Justice by seeking the acquittal of the innocent but never knowingly seeking the acquittal of the guilty.

Sometimes, unfortunately and inevitably, acting on one's instructions may be acting out a lie in that a client may be untruthful and acquittal may attend a lying and guilty client. These are occupational hazards not born of any dishonesty on the part of the Barrister but, for a lawyer, told by his client of his guilt, still to seek his acquittal runs contrary to the morality of a most honourable calling. Barristers must never prostitute their high calling in what would then be a perversion of the profession's high morality.

CHAPTER FIVE

Pupillage and Practice

When you start pupillage you begin a form of serfdom in which you literally do your pupilmaster's bidding. But the first six months of pupillage are crucial to later practice. Although you cannot take instructions in this first six months, you can not only watch and wait but you can try your hand at almost everything on your pupilmaster's table. If you are alert and persistent, you can get the feel of that strange phenomenon, Barristers' Chambers, learn that the Clerk is Lord and Master of all and learn to listen much but say nothing. You will learn that the Bar prostrates itself too much to instructing solicitors and you will learn to wait for your fees long after a case has been fought and won. And you will begin to learn of the straitjacket of etiquette and ethics which descends on you from your very first day. Dress and language, even private life, now need to be watched and some aspects of them curtailed. And if you have no work yourself then you are very much hostage to Fortune, who parades under the guise of the Clerk of Chambers. You learn to please and you are pleased to conform. But, to be fair, remembering that the Bar is the reservoir from which the judiciary is drawn, even I can concede that conformity need not destroy personality or individuality.

If your body has not been washed ashore at the end of your first six months then comes the time of the first trials and tribulations because you can now go to court in your own right although still technically under pupillage. Before you go to court you should take every single brief to your pupilmaster and get his advice on any aspects which worry you. Pupillage must not be used for learning your trade over the imprisoned bodies of your lay clients! Courtwork is a deadly serious business, certainly for the client whose neck may be on the chopping-block. You will learn in these few months that the barrister can be barrister, confidante, friend, sociologist, psychologist, social worker, anything you wish to those in need before the criminal courts. The task is not only one of law and advocacy but of understanding, awareness and sympathy. The test you should learn is the test of how the client feels at the end of it all, win or lose. There is far too much playing around with the liberty of the subject by greedy Clerks who send unready pupils to cases as yet beyond their ability and experience; if you do not feel up to a case, consult your pupilmaster; if you still feel unready, refuse to trifle with the client's liberty.

Your second six months should begin with matters of remands, bail applications, pleas in mitigations and committals where the risks are minimal. A pupil should be left with uncontested matters and trials should never be left to him unless the pupilmaster is absolutely sure of his readiness; a hard decision if the case has to go elsewhere but a high standard at the beginning is right and proper. Remember always, it's not your neck on the block, it's your client's neck!

It is deemed automatic at the Bar that a pupil at the end of his twelve months' pupillage is a fit and proper person to become a tenant and an independent practitioner in his own right. The evidence suggests that more than half of the annual pupil intake at the Bar should never be allowed to practise and no pupils should ever be granted tenancies unless pupilmasters can state in writing to the Senate that they truly recommend that such pupil should now proceed to practice. It seems to me that the Inns of Courts should require from all pupilmasters such a Certificate of Competence. This should be a solemn declaration and should be signed by Pupilmaster, Head of Chambers and the Clerk. This most necessary filter will stop at source those clearly not well-equipped for the profession. The Bar, with sweet perversity, is now asking for secret certificates "of attitudes" from tutors at universities and colleges of law at a time when the potential aspirant has yet had no chance to prove himself. The time for vetting is at the end of the twelve months of full pupillage and not before or after. If no such solemn declaration is forthcoming then the potential practitioner must seek periods of extended pupillage until he can acquire such solemn recommendation.

The question of finding a place in Chambers will continue to be a source of frustration for many since recent reports of the Advisory Committee on Legal Education have recommended that the Bar School of Law only take in 600 students every year with the possibility of only 300 entering practice. There is strain and stress at the Bar now against allowing the entry of radicals and dissidents and the secret reports called for from the universities are designed to weed out such "troublemakers". Places in Chambers will now be available to the

conformists and to the conventional; they will be denied to the radical
and, of course, to some blacks. The Bar is moving to the right! Add to
this the new rules that state that no barrister may set up Chambers
outside premises owned or managed by the Inns of Court without
express permission of the Bar Committee and you will see that
geographical limits are now to be added to secret reports to keep the
Bar small and conservative.

Once you get a tenancy then starts the business of paying a fixed
rent and of handing over a fixed percentage of your earnings to your
Clerk, usually ten per cent. You will have your own desk and your
briefs and correspondence will be placed on your desk. You are
though effectively a tenant at will and very much subject to being
ejected by the Head of Chambers if relationships go wrong. So there is
still much need for cordiality, if not docility.

Relations in Chambers are very much an intimate thing in that you
need to get on with the others on a reasonably friendly basis, if only
because you will need to depend on other people's solicitors for your
work. Senior members of Chambers are always available however to
advise you and to discuss points of law with you and you should lean
heavily upon them. After the first year of practice the shape of things
to come will become less blurred and you will be able to perceive and
understand the nature of the profession and the methods of practice.
But a lot will still depend on how you perform when on your own feet,
very lonely feet, in a court of law and now we will turn to that.

CHAPTER SIX

You and Instructing Solicitors

Counsel has to rely on instructing solicitors for every material assistance concerned with the trial and you are only allowed to become involved in a case where the lay client has seen and instructed solicitors and where the brief finds its way on to your desk via your Clerk of Chambers. Long before you are asked to advise solicitors and client the case may have been won or lost by solicitors' diligence or lack of it since, unless you yourself did the committal for trial, solicitors will have done the preparation themselves and you may be faced at short notice with a badly prepared brief. This is particularly dangerous in cases where notice of alibi has to be given and has not been done; so the first lesson is to open every single brief the moment it lands on your desk and check the preparation of the defence and advise in writing within the first twenty-four hours of receipt. The quicker you advise the longer warning you give and the better basis to ask for postponement of trial if required.

By and large, with some distinguished exceptions the competence of solicitors in the criminal courts leaves much to be desired. As I say, their real job is preparation which involves the finding of witnesses for defendants who are often in custody. There are too many lazy solicitors, who, if the client is in custody, yet expect the client to get his witnesses to the solicitor's office by his own efforts rather than the solicitor walking the streets himself.

A lot of solicitors, especially those set up conveniently right opposite the magistrates courts, get their work too easily. A lot of their work comes to them through the court itself and not through the client directly and for this reason the beneficiary solicitors are never anxious to rock the gravy boat. Some solicitors even get "recommendations" from police or prison officers! This kind of Legal Aid "handout" is dangerous not only to the commitment of defence solicitors but because it places a dangerous weapon of patronage in the hands of the local courts who are able to fill in the names of solicitors when the client does not know of one. A careful scrutiny of the allocation of Legal Aid certificates to certain firms will show that patronage and preference exists and this must dilute and sap the commitment to justice of certain favoured firms. The situation becomes particularly dangerous if the client on his first morning after arrest finds himself in the care of the Duty Solicitor of the day and then, when he turns to a solicitor of his own choice thereafter, the court refuses to allow the changeover requested by him. The Duty Solicitor Scheme therefore can create a colonising influence on the minds (and purses!) of local solicitors in that the court is seen to protect and prefer those having connections with the court. This can make heavy inroads on the fundamental right that the citizen is free to choose his own lawyer so that it becomes one law (or solicitor) for the rich and one for the poor (or legally aided person). Solicitors of course have "favourite" barristers and unless they allow their client freedom of choice of Counsel then he is inevitably saddled with Counsel imposed on him. As I say, the situation is seen in its true context when one examines the freedom of choice always afforded the rich man as against the legally aided one.

Counsel should insist that the client be asked not only for a full statement of his own version of events on the charges that he faces but also his most detailed comments and critique on every single prosecution witness. Wherever the client mentions the possibility of a defence witness then Counsel must advise the interviewing of that witness. By the time Counsel sees the client in conference the solicitor should have interviewed every single potential defence possible and placed the fruits of such interviews with Counsel's papers. Far too often Counsel is assailed with witness statements in the middle of a trial. This means that he has never had the chance to put the evidence of that witness in contradiction of the prosecution. If a defence exists then the quicker it is prepared the better. Recent witnesses recently acquired are often seen as the product of recent invention!

CHAPTER SEVEN

Challenging the Jury

By the time you reach the Court of Trial and the trial judge orders the panel of jurors to be brought into court you will have advised your client and solicitors on the evidence, including the possibility of offering lesser pleas and the area of evidence offered in respect of each contested charge. You will therefore know the size and scope of the challenge of the prosecution case. You will know further the type of case it is and you should know the type of jurors you would like to achieve through exercising your right of challenge. For example, barrister Sibghat Kadri once took the view that he would like to have an all-female jury in an Old Bailey rape trial and that all-female jury eventually acquitted. Some barristers never challenge at all and generally speaking the convention is not to challenge. But there are cases where jurors must be challenged!

In the Bristol Riots case, exercising the right of collective peremptory challenge brought in five black jurors to join seven whites to try 12 blacks charged with riot and that jury acquitted. Lord Denning castigated the defence lawyers who challenged to get the blacks on and he said "that jury so constituted went on to acquit the real troublemakers." Such absolute and racist rubbish to fall from such a distinguished source, in the sense that he could not himself begin to know who "the real troublemakers" were, he did not listen to the jury's deliberations and he did not hear the evidence. Added to which the jury were unanimous in their acquittal and so the seven whites must also have agreed to acquit. But Lord Denning did not challenge the integrity of the seven whites! What is undoubtedly true is that blacks on such juries bring an air of reality to heavy allegations against police launched by black defendants. In the trial of the Cricklewood 12 (the police raid on the Carib Club) the four blacks on that jury undoubtedly played important parts in the acquittals which followed but not because of lack of honesty but because blacks know what blacks experience. In the trial of the Leeds Bonfire 10 challenges were made to ensure youth on the jury and in the Trial of the Bradford 12 and the Newham 8 applications were made to get Asian jurors. And why not? If your client is tried by his peers and if his defence involves the making of racist remarks by police officers to him then blacks are essential on that jury.

In the rape trial of Peter Smith where a fifteen-year old girl alleged rape and a doctor gave evidence of an unbroken hymen women were specifically kept on by the defence. Horses for courses every time. Smith was found "not guilty!"

And yet the judiciary in England continues to make faces whenever application is made for juries that reflect a cross-section of society. And one suspects the nastiest things go on in the Lord Chancellor's Department at Cardiff Crown Court where people from the Docks area are never to be found on jury panels!

Jury trial involves consideration of all the issues by twelve fellow citizens, biases, prejudices, warts and all and it is both sad and true that one jury would convict and another acquit the same client on the same evidence. But luckily for the astute defence Counsel potential jurors wear their prejudices on their sleeves, in their dress, in their haircuts, in the newspaper folded under their arms and, most importantly, in the very set of their face; these matters tell a lot and the exercise of the right of peremptory challenge with some skill can yield rich rewards. The exercise of this right has been ridiculed of late but only because it has fallen into disuse and so is fair game for attack; but the recent list of black civil liberties trials revived its use. Do not be put off by a glaring judge, you go ahead and exercise your client's statutory right of challenge!

Having decided what kind of jurors you want you will view swiftly what is on offer on the panel and use your challenges accordingly. At the end of the day you have to look twelve people straight in the eyes and convince them of the innocence of your client; if, for any reason, conscious or not, you do not feel you can communicate your client's innocence with one particular face, challenge! In using the right of challenge you will bear in mind the dimensions of conflict in the case and if there be any allegations of prejudice or perjury. Generally speaking, young jurors believe accusations against the police more easily than old jurors. Generally speaking, women are the best judges of another woman's rape complaint. Generally speaking, the long-haired, the bearded and the scruffily-dressed, those wearing CND or Troops Out labels are the best bet for the defence. Nonconformity for the defence, conformity for the prosecution.

When considering this question of challenge remember that the court in the U.S.A. trying black radical Angela Davis spent three days examining jury challenges. Yet in England we are looked on with disapproval if we do. Jury challenge for prejudice should be allowed in the U.K. on the same basis that it is allowed in the U.S.A. Every man has his prejudices and his bias and there cannot be fair trial if the defence are in ignorance of such attitudes. Once again, clear evidence that the American courts are more realistic than our own.

CHAPTER EIGHT

Cross-Examination: General Matters

The most important aspect of the conduct of the defence in the criminal trial is the ability of Counsel for the defence to cross-examine with perception and penetrative power to the destruction or reduction of the prosecution case. Some barristers' cross-examinations are born in a Mayfair drawing room, other people's are born in the ghettoes. Background and associations give perception. Sympathy with the client's condition gives added thrust. Anger with injustice give Cruise Missile lift-off! Hatred of corrupt prosecutions gives Exocet-style destructive power!

The first hint about cross-examination in the criminal courts is to try and assess the integrity and general credibility of the witness in the eyes of the jury as they first give evidence. The crucial question will always be: How well is that witness coming over to the jury? Is his evidence, as yet untested, sounding credible? If it's a young girl giving evidence of rape, is she cool and clinical or nervous or embarrassed? If it's her mother giving evidence about her daughter is she prone to exaggerate or to go off at a tangent? Where are the conflicts between her evidence and your client's case? Which evidence is more realistic?

Your view of the witness will obviously be coloured by the face that your client has given you certain instructions as to whether this witness is lying or telling the truth. Counsel's first appraisal will be of the relevance and weight of the evidence. For a witness may give only marginal evidence, e.g. about the precise time of a robbery which may or may not be of a contested nature or, to quote another example, the witness may give evidence of a robbery but may not give evidence which links the defendant with the crime.

The very first lesson for the young Clarence Darrow to learn is never to ask questions unnecessarily. If the evidence does not incriminate your client then don't tempt Fate – shut up and sit tight.

It may well be a case where grave allegations have to be made against some witnesses but not against others. Those witnesses whose evidence is accepted or only marginally disputed or does not in any significant way incriminate the defendant can be met with great courtesy to provide the great contrast for the jury when comparing and contrasting the blitzkrieg you have to launch against another witness.

The object of cross-examination is to destroy the lying witness and to test the reliability of others whose evidence is disputed but against whom no charges of dishonesty can properly be made. There will be witnesses who need be asked only for clarification of their evidence. There are others who may be challenged gently or on grounds of honest mistake.

There are three fundamental rules which the practitioner should have in mind at all times during cross-examination: Firstly, how relevant is the evidence against your client on the charges as listed? It may be relevant against a co-defendant but not against your own client so please do learn to shut up and not ask questions for the sake of asking.

Secondly, how important is the evidence, i.e. is it sink-or-swim evidence or is it evidence which can be nebulous or vague or can cut both ways? When civilian witnesses in the Islington 18 trial came along to testify that they were robbed by a number of unknown blacks in a series of robberies at the Notting Hill Carnival, while the identities of the robbers were crucial, the fact that these strangers to the defence had been robbed at the date, time and place they said could not possibly be challenged. Here again, unless it is to seek clarification on the height, hairstyle, dress and other accompanying descriptions which may contradict your client's appearance and description and therefore help in contesting police "confessions" by your client, ask questions with caution.

The third matter is this: What does your client say about the evidence? Cross-examination as it proceeds may bring other matters into the case. A cross-examination, for example, which attacks the character and integrity of prosecution witnesses may "let in" the previous criminal record of the accused. Again, cross-examination of a co-defendant, whose alleged confessions not in the presence and hearing of your own client cannot be evidence against your defendant, can become evidence if you cross-examine the co-defendant in such a way that he there and then adopts the entirety of his confessions as he gives evidence in open court. There is also the danger of defence Counsel asking "one question too many", i.e. not knowing when to sit down. Eric Crowther, now Mr. Recorder Crowther QC, was always fond of telling the story against himself when he was representing a client charged with stealing £500 in cash from another person. Crowther in cross-examination put his client's case of denial and asked questions tending to suggest that the witness could never possibly walk around with that amount of cash upon his person. So far so good, had the cross-examination ended there. But he went on to ask that "one question too many" which was "Do you happen to have such an amount in cash on you at this moment?" in suitably sarcastic tone. Whereupon, as he tells it, the witness replied "Well, now that you ask me, I just happen to have over £1,000 in cash upon me," and the witness then produced a large bundle of notes! Many a time have defence barristers strengthened the case for the prosecution by rambling on when they should be shutting up. There was the case of the Villa Cross 7 at Birmingham Crown Court when a barrister for the defence (who shall be nameless!) disputed police evidence that photographs taken of alleged drug peddlers showed his client in the act of selling. The photographs would not normally have been admissible in evidence but Counsel went on to challenge the witness: "Are you saying that these photographs exist and can be brought before this jury?" The witness answered in the affirmative, the photographs were brought and showed his client in the most incriminating situations and that was the beginning of the end.

How relevant is the evidence?

Many a time and oft defence barristers embark on excursions into areas of evidence not really helpful to the jury's determination of the evidence and waste not only time but juristic energy which they should indeed be helping to conserve for the real moments of concentration on the real issues of the case. If the evidence does not move the case against or for one's client LEAVE IT ALONE and go on to matters that do. Nothing so distracts a jury as irrelevant cross-examination and nothing is more calculated to drive a judge to the other side of dementia. Some evidence may be marginal and some may be vital, and there are many grey areas of evidence in between; much skill is required in attaching only that importance to the evidence which it truly deserves when viewed in the overall context of the fundamental issues.

What does the defendant say about the evidence?

First lesson is, if your client does not challenge the evidence, neither can you. If he admits being in a certain place at a certain time but merely disputes the company he was with, make it clear from your very first words, please, that you accept the first two matters and only challenge the third. This makes for simplicity and much saving of time. Basically, it must be remembered that in the preparation of cross-examination the source, nature and content of the cross-examination all originate from the defendant's instructions. The defendant knows best the truth or not of the matters alleged against him. He knows whether the police officers in the case are telling the whole truth, part of the truth, or no truth at all. Cross-examination must be nailed firmly to the floor of the client's instructions and must not wander around without such firm and clear support. There is of course another source of cross-examination and that is where uncontested evidence is adduced and then the defence is entitled to adopt such evidence if it wishes. In the trial of the Cricklewood 12, evidence was given by prosecution witnesses that the doorman at Willesden's Carib Club was knocked flying down the stairs with the striking officers allegedly saying to him: "You're fucking sacked tonight!" In this context, the defence extracted and adopted this evidence and made it part of its own case since the incident of police assault was relevant to the issue of affray as charged.

In the trial of Donat Smith (see Who Killed Maureen Armstrong? by Rudy Narayan),the evidence of the prosecution witness Miss B that she had been beaten up by police officers before changing her story about the movements of the accused was first extracted and then adopted by the defence as their own case in launching an attack on the police corruption in the case.

In the trial of the Stockwell 10, the evidence of a prosecution witness that London Transport police had themselves brought a tube train to a grinding halt at Stockwell underground was adopted by the defence in seeking to establish its case of police entrapment preceding assault. In the trial of the Thornton Heath 15, the evidence of prosecution witnesses that members of the Croydon National Front had rioted against the blacks prior to any response from the defendant was adopted by the defence as relevant to the issue of self-defence before the jury.

Counsel for the Defence will of course have a proof of evidence from the client coupled with witness statements which will be more or less supportive of his client's case. He will have in addition the most total and comprehensive commentary by his client of the prosecution case. In addition he will have copies of the previous criminal record of his client and of any defence witnesses (and the prosecution are under a duty to supply the defence with copies of the previous record of every prosecution witness). There is one area, however, which has brought too many Defence Counsel, brilliant and not so brilliant, sprawling flat on their faces before many a jury and that is the area where the defence witness has already been interviewed by the police and has said in that interview or written statement things which contradict his present intended evidence and which may even agree with the prosecution case. In the murder trial of Clarence Reuben Smith, the defence (led by the distinguished George Shindler QC as he then was) advanced the proposition that the defendant Rutherford had been attacked by the victim, his then tenant, downstairs in the kitchen and he then had only acted on the spur of the moment in self-defence. However, this defence version was not supported by a written statement Smith's wife had already made to Brixton police and instructing solicitors had neglected to ask her about this previous statement. Mrs Smith, of course, being the wife of the defendant, was not a compellable witness by the prosecution but, when she was called by the defence, the prosecution, in the elegant, smooth-smiling form of Brian Leary QC, was entitled to put to her this previous statement which not only contradicted the defence case but supported the prosecution allegations.

Police enquiries are usually much wider than the depositions reveal and while the prosecution is obliged to supply the defence with material which may assist the defence they are not in any way obliged to reveal the deadly contradictory versions which friends or relatives of the defendant may have given as part of police enquiries. This area is a veritable minefield and you should advise your solicitors to cross-examine every single defence witness as to the existence and content of such statements.

By the time the defence barrister, armed with all the above, meets his client in pre-trial conference, he will already be fashioning the shape and structure of his cross-examination; by this time, both he and his client will be well aware of the strengths and weaknesses of his case. This is the telling time when the defence barrister will, after considering the evidence, the client's proof of evidence, the client's commentary on the prosecution case, defence witness statements, criminal record of all concerned and information about any contradictory witness statements made to police, decide upon the kind of cross-examination relevant to the defence in that particular case. Mentioning previous convictions of prospective defence witnesses reminds me of the trial of Jefferson Smith in the Cardiff Crown Court when defence Counsel called for the previous criminal records of all such witnesses. One such witness, provisionally called to contradict the prosecution evidence of a point-blank nightclub shooting, had a previous conviction for perverting the course of justice! Needless to say, this witness was dropped like the proverbial brick!

So the question is, what kind of cross-examination are you going to employ in a particular case?

CHAPTER NINE

Cross-Examining Upon the Evidence

The Prosecution will call its evidence-in-chief and Counsel for the Defence will then have to test that evidence for honesty, reliability and, hopefully, elicit certain contradictions.

But, even before the Defence Barrister begins to cross-examine he will have been able to assess those parts of the prosecution case which, viewed as facts, cannot be disputed or denied. Such facts include, at their simplest, photographs and plans of the scene of the crime, medical reports and scientific evidence, the latter two being usually reliable and such expert witnesses being only asked to attend to clarify some obscure point. There are other parts of the evidence, date, time and place of the crime, which are clearly common ground and would be a waste of public time and money to pursue in evidence. Formal admissions by the defence can save much time and energy.

There also exists in many cases the facts leading up to the crime alleged – such facts which merely set the scene can usually be "led" by the prosecution or the witness statements read. For example, in very many robbery cases, in which a stolen motor car has been used, evidence from the owner as to the existence and identity of such car and the date, time and place in which it was last left by him can be read from statements.

Counsel for the Defence is then faced with the facts alleged as the basis of the offence seeking to link its client with the crime charged.

There is a certain line of cases where the facts as alleged cannot be disputed but it either falls short of linking the defendant with the crime itself or the facts are otherwise inadequate in law to the full satisfaction of all the necessary ingredients of the crime. In the trial of Donat Smith there could be no doubt that the crime of murder was committed by someone. But what was found wanting was the link with the defendant through the medium of alleged confession by him. In the murder/affray case of Anforah Jones the question was whether an affray had actually been committed as a matter of law, because if terror be the absent ingredient from fighting in the streets then the charge cannot be made out as a matter of law even though the defendant was an admitted participant in incidents in a public place.

Cross-examination in these instances is confined and directed towards submission before the trial judge that the legal ingredients of the charge are not fully made out. This kind of cross-examination is very much the cool, clinical, scientific kind, aimed as it is at the judicial mind and not at the jury. If the submission fails as a matter of law it still does not prevent Counsel advancing robust submissions to the jury in the most rhetorical terms!

CHAPTER TEN

Cross-Examination: Gathering Ammunition

It happens in certain cases that prosecution witnesses can be made to contradict each other in such a confusing way that the jury is left at the end of the day with at least three or four possibilities.

The Trial of the Bristol 12 was a classic of its kind and the cross-examination that set alleged riot-leader Franklyn Brown free was copybook stuff of its kind. The prosecution had called a number of police officers to testify as to the riotous activities of the man in the blue tracksuit. What usually happens in cases with a large number of defendants charged with public order offences like riot and affray is that police officers are paired off, two to each defendant. In Brown's case there were about six police officers who came to testify against him and, if believed, he would most certainly have been convicted for riot. Unfortunately for this unhappy prosecution, there were also at least another ten police officers called, but ostensibly to deal with the alleged rioting of other defendants. They did not even mention Brown in their evidence. But Defence Counsel, probing gently at first as he stood at the top of the precipice, first established that certain officers knew Brown by face and by name. He then got these same officers to admit that they had never seen Brown do anything wrong. Further, he then secured admissions from the police officers that there was no "man in a blue tracksuit" at any point at which Brown was alleged to have been rioting. Armed with this divisive cross-examination, it was but a short step to acquittal. And, while police officers had testified to the general riot, every single civilian witness called for the prosecution, cross-examined by Brown's counsel, effectively testified to the effect that if anyone had rioted then it must have been the police and not the civilians at St. Paul's Black and White Cafe!

So that in some cases, it is possible to gather ammunition from one section of prosecution witnesses to use against another group. In nearly every single public order case in the criminal courts civilian evidence can be made to contradict police evidence to the advantage of the Defence. Gathering ammunition therefore is gathering contradictions from one set of prosecution witnesses to use against another. Counsel for the defence should always be alert and astute to the possibilities of contradiction and the area most likely to assist his client.

Another example of gathering ammunition was in the Trial of the Metro 4, the Old Bailey affray trial which followed upon the siege of the Metro Youth Club in London's Notting Hill. Prosecution witnesses had alleged that the black youth Howard Green, armed with a hammer, had literally run amok among legions of police officers and laid officers low to his left and to his right as he performed a world beating rugby-style weaving action in and among their ranks. Various officers were alleged to have been hammered to the ground by him in precise and particular sequence, the direction and location of each flooring being established vis-à-vis the street geography and vis-à-vis other people.

Defence Counsel therefore invited the police witnesses, in turn, to mark on a blank street plan the places where the witnesses stated that Green had struck particular blows. The witnesses each marked the location on fresh and clean plans. All the witnesses placed the acts of assault as happening at different places. All twenty-four counts in the indictment were thrown out by the jury!

Defence Barristers therefore need to be on the look-out in every case for ammunition that comes from the mouth of prosecution witnesses. If the contradiction and conflict comes from the prosecution witnesses as opposed to the defence then it has added weight with the jury since the prosecution cannot both rely on their own witnesses and throw the offending ones overboard. Gathering ammunition therefore is potentially an exercise that can blow many prosecutions to bits.

CHAPTER ELEVEN

Cross-Examination: The Blitz

There are some cases in the criminal courts where the defendant positively alleges that the police have deliberately and falsely sought to manufacture false evidence against him, in a word, that they are trying to frame him on that charge. In some cases, like the trial of Donat Smith, the trial of Christopher Smith, the trial of Anforah Jones, the defendant may be facing a multiplicity of charges including murder and may well have a previous criminal record which could be massively prejudicial to his interests if disclosed to a trial jury. This poses a serious problem for his Defence Barrister because grave charges carry grave risk of heavy sentences and such attacking defences inevitably let his previous record in before the jury. So that the risks are great all round and the defence has to be very bold indeed to launch such attack.

It may be, for example, that even such a case can be fought on the basis of "honest mistake" on the part of an officer arresting and charging an innocent man. But where an innocent man is charged upon mistake the picture is usually clear, e.g. the charging by Putney police of anti-apartheid campaigner Peter Hain for robbery of a Barclay's Bank; in this case it is very possible that the police acted reasonably on information supplied by others, i.e. by the schoolboy witnesses.

But if there has been a deliberate and lying conspiracy to frame an innocent man and this is self-evident from the client's instructions then the duty of the defence barrister is to put that defence fearlessly and coldbloodedly; and it is this duty of fearlessness in the teeth of convention that causes all the trouble. Some members of the English Bar flinch visibly at the sight and sound of a member of the Bar putting such a defence with vigour and, dare I say it, with open enjoyment even. Not only do they, generally speaking, shrink from advancing such defences but they consciously avoid the company of those who do. And there are regrettably a number of cases in which even Queen's Counsel have refused to advance such strong defences although it is true to say that the situation is now changing for the better.

Certainly one can agree that it is a matter of tactics to be considered as to whether the case can be fought to success with this type of blitzkrieg cross-examination and advocacy, but the fact remains that Counsel is bound by his intructions and he has the highest duty to put them, no matter what it costs him personally either in terms of judicial displeasure or police animosity. If Defence Barristers will not stand up and fight for the citizen client against corrupt police then the profession ought to disbar itself in total disgrace.

But the Blitz can only be mounted when one's gunpowder is absolutely dry and preferably when one has an ample supply of such gunpowder. For the Blitz is the sudden, immediate and total launching (in the very first moments of cross-examination) of an all-out attack on the prosecution case as a frame-up by police officers. And the first questions cannot be veiled, they must be totally naked in their splendour. This is the bold approach and not for those of nervous dispositions; the stakes are high and the Blitz eminently nerve-racking on both sides. It "ups" the stakes to fever pitch.

It pays dividends in that the jury know right from the start exactly how the case is being put up. The jury is tuned to the defence wavelength from the start. There is nothing ambiguous about the first question in cross-examination being phrased as follows: "Detective Chief Superintendent Smith, I suggest you have come here to tell a pack of lies."

Put with brutal resonance it opens up a course from which there is no turning back. For this reason, Blitz-style cross-examination must be supported by the most vigorous and analytical approach and backed up by solid, reliable, accurate and truthful defence witnesses on crucial issues. Nothing is more pitiful that great allegations loudly put, only to fall foul of the quicksands of lying defence witnesses.

One of the first examples of Blitz-style cross-examination was in the re-trial at the Old Bailey of the Cricklewood 3 (9 of the original 12 having been acquitted first time round). Oliver Smith, a youth of good character, alleged that the officer in the case had first asked him to say that: "Dennis Bovell (later to found Matumbi the musical group) spoke on the microphone" and that Smith, when he refused, was then told he would himself be put on an identification parade and that, said the officer, "You will be picked out anyway." There were other supports for Smith's defence in that the doorman Henry Brooks had claimed that he was thrown down the stairs by police and told as he tumbled: "You're fucking sacked tonight!"

Evidence was also available that police officers had lined the stairs at the Carib Club and waited there with their own drawn truncheons. And there was evidence of blacks being beaten up, racially abused and thrown over railings into police vans. And there was more. There was in this case all the explosive ingredients, backed up by medical evidence, for a full scale, non-stop Blitz on the reeling prosecution. A similar military operation was carried out in the Trials of the Metro Four, the Leeds 10 and the Islington 18.

While the Blitz is a weapon that can carry all before it, it cannot be mounted except upon firm instructions supported by the strongest and most reliable evidence. For the effect of the Blitz is to turn the tables upon the enemy and effectively put the prosecution themselves on trial. It is the largest single weapon of proven defence in the arsenal of the black political case but cannot be brought out except when the battlefield has been most clearly mined for the enemy's advance.

Chapter Twelve

Cross-Examination: Back to the Wall

There are cases of course where the evidence against the defendant is absolutely overwhelming and where verdicts of Guilty are merely a matter of time, yet the defendant wishes to advance a lying defence even in the face of certain annihilation.

Where the evidence against the defendant is overwhelming – so much so that his own barrister would convict him – then, nothwith-standing one's instructions, it is the duty of honourable Counsel to advise his client as to the hopelessness of his position should he wish to contest the matter, and to the possibilities of a lenient sentence if he pleads. This is in no way to abdicate one's duty to defend but one's duty does not include prostitution of the role of advocate and it is in no way treacherous to so advise the client.

If, having been given strong advice and faced with such evidence, the client still insists on contesting the charges then his Barrister is in a difficult position. Counsel is not allowed to advocate a trial where a client has confided his guilt but if a client insists on fighting the trial then Counsel must do his duty. This becomes a delicate situation because although Counsel's duty is to fight the case and put his client's instructions he has also, as another duty to his client, to "Keep one eye on the sentence." The Blitz method will clearly not do in this position ... the method employed is more aptly titled the Back to the Wall position. For example, where fingerprints upon the murder weapon are proved to be those of your client, where the victim's rare blood group is found in your client's bedroom, where your client has confessed in writing in the presence of and after advice from his solicitor or father, where there is identification at the scene of the crime by people who know him, then it is tempting fate, without support from the strongest scientific or alibi evidence, to allege that the entire prosecution is a concoction.

In this situation, one can only do one's best to elicit factors of mitigation to be used in due course. But is is an area of great delicacy and junior practitioners should not be burdened with such impossible defences.

CHAPTER THIRTEEN

Cross-Examination: Putting One's Case

Cross-Examination can be divided into two stages, the first being to test the evidence of the prosecution but the other, equally important, is to put your client's case by making positive and clear suggestions to the witness. Sometimes these suggestions can be doubled up with the enquiring question, the suggestion merely being "I suggest that my client did not say these words to you." But what happens if your client has given you an alternative version to that which the prosecution witness has testified to? Then your duty is to suggest: "I suggest to you that what he truly said was ..."

This duty to put one's client's case could be extremely vivid or extremely tedious, in that one can put with flair and style: "I suggest that you then punched my client in the face." But when your client denies page after page of police "verbals" in an interview then all of it has to be specifically denied. If your client simply denies what effectively appears on pages 3 to 8 of the officer's deposition then one can short-circuit the operation by putting simply a blanket denial of the contents of those pages. But if your client offers alternative answers to most of those recorded then they must be put with clarity and precision. All this detail slows the action down of course and is bad for dynamics. To speed up the dynamics one puts the tedious bits first to get it out of the way and on the record, and then one can revel again in sinking one's fangs into the putting of more vivid allegations.

Judges rightly get very impatient with Counsel who put denials but do not put their client's case. It is said that witnesses are entitled to have allegations put to them so that they might answer but it is equally useful that the jury knows how long before the client steps into the witness box what his answer is to all that is said against him. In a huge number of cases the prosecution version of events differs from the defence's and where this is so Defence Counsel will obviously test the matters which the defence denies and refutes. But the jury is greatly assisted if the case for the defence is incorporated into the body of the first main cross-examination so that the issues come alive early on in the trial. Cleverly used, "putting the case" for the defence can also assist the jury by "narrowing the issues" so that the area of jury concentration is narrowed down immediately. If the jury is concentrating on whether the prosecution case is wholly true, partly true or not true at all, not "putting the case" deprives them of that vital contrast and comparison against which to consider defence allegations and assertions.

"Putting the case" also has the psychological value of turning the tables on the prosecution since the defence is now taking to the offensive. A classic example of "Putting the case" was with the instance of Leon Johnson at Manchester Crown Court; even though the charge was slight, the lesson is there to be learnt. A man called Berry, the defendant's friend, had been called to testify that the defendant was the driver of a car that had been driven off without paying.

Johnson's defence was that it was Berry who had stolen the petrol and had even asked Johnson to plead Guilty and that he, Berry, would then pay the fine. Berry was cross-examined on the evidence only at first to establish the limits of his evidence and then Johnson's case was put in the clearest terms.

That way the jury was appraised in precise manner of the 'alternative possibilities" as to the identity of the petrol thief.

It was also "put" to the police that Johnson had offered a number of alibi witnesses as to his whereabouts at the material time. It was also "put" that he had offered a reward if the petrol attendant could identify him. It was also "put" that Johnson was a local community leader who had made many complaints against local police and that it was only after he wrote to the Chief Constable complaining about the officers on the enquiry that he was then charged. Thus, during the course of cross-examination, the entire defence case was placed before the jury. Johnson was acquitted! It is vital that the defence case be placed in this way before the jury at the earliest moment that cross-examination allows.

Chapter Fourteen

Cross-Examination: Talking to the Jury

The formal occasions afforded Defence Counsel for addressing the jury are when he opens and closes his case. The Opening Speech is merely to outline the defence and to draw, in advance of the evidence, the salient features of such defence to the jury's attention although it is quite legitimate to use one's opening speech to castigate several, or all, aspects of the prosecution case that has just ended. The closing speech is the time to analyse the evidence on both sides and to marshall the arguments that can be honestly and realistically advanced to secure the defendant's acquittal.

In practice however, these formal addresses are never quite so effective as they are intended to be. Generally speaking, the battle has been won and lost long before Counsel's closing speech to the jury, again generally speaking, it is cross-examination that wins and loses cases.

Cross-examination can be the most devastating and effective way of talking to the jury since tone of voice, gestures, inflexions, calculated timing and skilled phrasing can convey so much in questions which, although never agreed to by the witness, nevertheless "bounce off" the witness and on to the jury. Of course, questions asked in cross-examination are really to elicit answers contradicting the prosecution case or assisting the defence position.

But questions can be asked in a dead, flat, boring monotone that conveys nothing except Hamlet's "words, words, words" while voice projection, the calculated phrase, a sense of timing and the shrewdest use of incredulity can make the question more important than the answer. For example, in the trial of the Cricklewood 12, the following questions were asked and answered as follows:

(It is important to note that the charge was affray and that the defence was that police officers had offered the first violence and that if anyone had caused an affray in the club that night it was police not black youths. You will see that the questions were not only designed to be more important than the answers but that the cross-examiner knew in advance what the answer would be before he asked the question. This is a minor classic in so far as it established the defence neatly and swiftly.)

Question: Did there come a time when police officers were lined up and down the stairs?

Answer: "Yes, sir."

Question: Were the officers lined up on both sides of the staircase?

Answer: "Yes, sir."

Question: Were they, as they were so lined up, within arm's reach of each other?

Answer: "Yes, sir."

Question: Were those officers in possession of truncheons?

Answer: "Yes, Sir."

Question: Were they lined up on the stairs from the very top to the very bottom?

Answer: "Yes, Sir."

Question: At this time when they were so lined up, was there then the slightest violence on the stairs, perhaps caused by police?

Answer: "No, sir. No violence at all."

Question: And so, we can agree this, before a single act of violence on those stairs, police were lined up on both sides?

Answer: "Yes, sir."

Question: With truncheons?

Answer: "Yes, sir."

Question: Doing nothing, simply waiting?

Answer: "Yes, sir."

Question: Waiting for the youths?

Answer: "Yes, sir."

In the above extract, all the evidence came through ten questions asked, the witness merely providing confirmation. It is an open secret that an element of bluff is involved since the questions must be put in such a way that forces the witness to answer truthfully.

It is this type of cross-examination that allows Defence Counsel to talk to the jury long before the final address comes. Counsel has in effect dictated the style, phrasing and impact of the evidence which he will later quote to the jury in his final speech.

Looks, glances tell a whole story and, mixed in the right ingredients and accompanied by a splendid sense of timing and relevance, can make a particularly telling speech out of a short cross-examination. Put simply, every cross-examination is a minor speech to the jury and if questions are asked with vocal, even declamatory, emphasis you can stir the right responses from the jury. Trial by jury is an accumulation of mental and emotional responses that build up right through the trial and find consummation at the very end. By the time a trial reaches half-way there is no such thing as a jury with an open mind. The slide has already begun long before the defence case begins and that slide could then be going in either direction.

Chapter Fifteen

Cross-Examination: Observing the Jury

Jurors, like everyone else, react facially, with smirks, raised eye-
brows, whispered asides, exchanged glances, grimaces, notetaking,
the lot, all the time through the criminal trial and those reactions
should be utilised as early warning signs by defence barristers. Some
points in cross-examination or some answers given elicit certain
common responses from jurors, certain questions affect different
jurors in different but obvious ways.

It is extremely easy, as the case proceeds, for a careful and
systematic observation of any jury to reveal which jurors react
favourably or adversely to a given point. It is possible day by day,
witness by witness, to build up a "score" on which defence points
elicited favour, neutrality or even ridicule from certain jurors as the
case goes on.

Observing a jury is a painstaking and systematic task and there is no
guarantee that all reactions can be impeccably interpreted. (Just as
there is limited truth in the legend that convicting jurors never look at
the dock while an acquitting jury always does.) But careful and
studious annotation of certain jurors' responses to certain questions
and answers can reveal a rough but sometimes roughly accurate guide
as to the way the collective mind of a jury is working. This observation
of the jury can serve at least two purposes.

One purpose is the immediate function of assessing how one's case
is being received by the jury. The second spin-off reason is that it
assists the defence barrister in steering his ship clear of the obvious
rocks. It is a science that is totally new to the criminal courts but has
been used with great success in the black political trials.

Since careful observation allows one a rough idea of the strengths and weaknesses of one's case (as reflected in jury reactions) it also gives a good measure as to the possibility of taking a gamble in deciding impromptu and spontaneously whether to go for a witness in a quiet way or to launch an all-out attack. It is an area of the criminal trial that, coupled with the race, age group, occupation and class of jurors, is worthy of future serious research and analysis.

Chapter Sixteen

Cross-Examination: Putting the Defendant's Character in

This area of the criminal trial is a veritable minefield and many a defendant has been blown up by his character being carelessly, even negligently, allowed in before a jury by an incompetent Counsel.

If a firm and clear decision, agreed to by the client, has been made that everything, including the client's previous criminal record, will be tossed into the ring of trial then there can be no regrets since a course of all-out attack inevitably brings about that result. But, as a matter of tactics and jury psychology, it is then better for the previous criminal record to come voluntarily from the mouth of the accused as his defence barrister leads him in evidence-in-chief. The result, if convictions are put in by the defendant himself, is to reduce the otherwise dramatic and prejudicial effect such evidence would have if elicited by the prosecution. But it is a rare case that allows such a bold step and the matter should be given considerable thought and the defendant's consent expressly obtained before such a step is taken.

When a defendant in a criminal case attacks the character of the prosecution then the prosecution is allowed to attack the character of the defendant since the law says that a jury should be allowed to know the character of a defendant who launches such attacks.

If a defendant is a man who has never been convicted of crime in a court of law before then he has nothing to fear from launching such attack, but if he has a series of serious previous criminal convictions then it could in certain circumstances be suicidal. If, for example, a defendant is charged with rape and has previous convictions for rape or indecent assault then it is not very clever to fight the case in such a way that his character is let in, since such knowledge of previous conduct could operate to the massive prejudice of a fair trial. Unless of course a decision has been formally taken to let character in because the defence has to be conducted in a hostile and open way; hopefully the dangers have been carefully weighed before the decision was taken. But if the opposite is true – that is, that it has been clearly realised that to let character in is to let in the most dangerous prejudice – then the defence must be conducted with great care.

Whether or not the prosecution is allowed to elicit previous convictions of a defendant depends on how the defence has been conducted. For example, if in a rape case the defendant through his Counsel accuses the female complainant of "sleeping around", i.e. behaving like a prostitute (such cross-examination can now only be done with the judge's leave), that is an attack on the character of the complainant. The prosecution, in the discretion of the judge, would then be allowed to cross-examine the defendant on his own previous conduct, including previous convictions.

And it is not just such a point-blank attack that can bring these consequences. The state of the law now is such that if the defence amounts to the jury having to make a straight choice between whether the prosecution or the defence is lying, then that brings the situation within the discretion of the trial judge and it is only if he can be persuaded that the evidence is more prejudicial than probative that he will rule in the defendant's favour. Where, therefore, there exists the most damaging previous convictions, while matters must be put in denial and dispute, care must be taken not to use emotive words to the effect that the prosecution has fabricated the case against the defendant. In skating over such thin ice, Defence Counsel will have to be content with placing mere denial of matters alleged against his client.

It is a rule that is fraught with danger in that once a decision has been taken not to let character in then it deprives the defence of launching all-out attack in a dramatic and often devastating way on grounds of perjury, frame-up and fabrication. On the other hand, once such an attack is made then it must be clearly understood that there is no turning back.

It remains a decision of greatest importance and the situation where a defendant's previous record is "accidentally" let in should never be allowed to happen. It is a decision, of course, that should be taken well in advance of trial and dictates the strategy and tactics of cross-examination and the conduct of the whole defence and the very atmosphere of the trial. It should never be left until the day of the trial itself.

Chapter Seventeen

Cross-Examination: Putting Statements in

Witnesses for the Prosecution, when first seen by police officers with a view to their giving evidence, are invited to make written statements as to the evidence they can give. These statements are signed and dated under a statutory declaration to the effect that they can be prosecuted if they state therein anything they know to be false or do not believe to be true. This statement of the prosecution witness, along with other prosecution statements, is served upon the defence as part of the depositions or committal documents. It is on the basis of these collected statements that the committing magistrates court is invited to find that there is a case to be sent for trial, that, as lawyers put it, "there is a case to answer," i.e., that there is enough evidence revealed in the papers which require consideration by a jury and which require explanation by the defendant. These statements collectively form the basis for the prosecution on the particular charges laid against the defendant.

It is stressed immediately that these statements themselves are not "evidence" – a trial jury is not entitled to see them – the witness must give evidence "live" and be cross-examined upon that "live" evidence, except, of course, where the defence does not require the witness and the prosecution may then read the witness's statement by agreement; even with this agreement, while the contents of the statement are read the statement itself is never shown to the jury. The written statements are for the use of judge and Counsel only in following the sequence and content of the evidence and allowing judge and Counsel to see how far, if at all, the witness at trial departs from the statement he first made nearer to the time of the events referred to therein. But, it is repeated, such statements are not for the eyes of the jury. There is no trial by written statements.

There are, however, circumstances in which a statement may be shown to a jury and form part of the material which they are entitled to have before them when they consider their verdicts but, before this can happen, the statement has to be made an exhibit in the case and a proper formal procedure has first to be adopted.

The "putting in" of a statement lies almost exclusively in the hands of Counsel for the defence since it is only through his conduct of cross-examination that such statements can be exhibited in this way. Care and extreme caution must be exercised before exhibiting such statements.

There are occasions when previous inconsistent statements of a witness may be so put in to show that the witness has changed his story, is now lying or is generally not to be believed. For example, in the trial of Donat Smith a prosecution witness, Mrs. Christine Toolan, gave evidence that she had seen a black man answering the defendant's description driving a car, similar to the one he owned, in and around the streets where the murdered woman, Mrs. Maureen Armstrong, was last seen alive. This was vital evidence since the defendant always denied this. It transpired however that Mrs. Toolan had made a total of four statements on the very same topic, three statements being dated before the defendant's arrest and the fourth statement after his arrest.

The last and fourth statement was totally consistent with her evidence upon this point but examination of each of her three previous statements, all made nearer the time of the sightings she testified to, but each also preceding the defendant's arrest, made absolutely no mention of a man, black or white, being seen by her driving any kind of vehicle around that area on that particular night. The object of putting in her three previous statements was to establish that she had had three previous opportunities to tell of black men in cars on the night of the murder but had made no mention at all of this crucial matter. The three statements were therefore put in through cross-examination and exhibited, and formed part of the jury's bundle of exhibits in due course.

There is a set and definite procedure for putting statements in before a jury. The witness should be asked to look at his original statement and he may then, after identifying the statement, be shown a typewritten copy which is usually much easier to read. He should be asked to look at the date of the statement. He should be asked to identify his signatures at various places on the statement. He should be formally asked whether he accepts that that statement of that date and with his signatures is his statement. Once this procedure is gone through the defence, in seeking to establish contradiction between previous statement and present statement, may properly ask the judge to make the statement an exhibit. The contents of the statement, insofar as they contradict the testimony of the witness, may then be put to the witness.

The value of statements is only, of course, if they contradict present testimony. Statements by themselves do not add anything to a case if there be no contradiction between evidence and statement. But if there are important omissions from the previous statement that surely must be a matter which the jury can properly be entitled to consider on the question of whether the witness may have recently invented parts of his testimony adverse to the defence.

It should be noted that there is a world of difference between a witness's statement being exhibited as discussed above and a witness simply being invited to "refresh his memory" from a silent reading of his statement. A witness may give evidence, e.g., that he saw 100 people at a scene. The statement in which the event is recorded may state that he saw 20 people at the scene. The statement of course will have been made nearer to the time of the events alluded to therein and when details of the events must have been fresher in the witness's mind. It would be quite proper to invite the witness to look at his statement and "read it quietly over to yourself", i.e. to refresh his memory from his statement. He can then be asked the question again after he has had this chance of refreshing his memory in this way. If, despite his being shown the statement with its serious discrepancy on the question being asked, he still sticks to his testimony then consideration has to be given to the procedure of putting his statement in as an exhibit which contradicts his testimony, remembering always that while a statement so exhibited may be useful in contradiction of a particular point the same statement in other parts may be absolutely murderous on other aspects of the prosecution case! Even though a jury will be warned that statements are not evidence in themselves a jury will read the entire statement and there is no telling what effect the rest of the statement may have on their deliberations.

It is vital that the two matters be most carefully defined and distinguished so that statements are not "accidentally" put in by an incompetent Counsel who only seeks really to have the benefit of the witness refreshing his memory. It is worth repeating that the introduction of statements should be avoided unless Counsel is totally convinced that their introduction, taken as a whole documents, will help his case.

Chapter Eighteen

Cross-Examination of Co-defendants

When two or more co-defendants are being tried together counsel for the defence has to assess very early in the trial whether the defence of his client in any way contradicts or is likely to be contradicted by one or more co-defendants. If the co-defendant be friendly then there can be much common gain but if the co-defendant engages in what is termed a 'cut-throat' defence then mayhem and massacre may follow, not at the hands of the prosecution but at the hands of the co-defendants who may cross-examine as to previous convictions without being fettered by any of the rules that govern prosecution counsel's conduct in this area.

For example, in the Bristol Riots trial every defendant, apart from contesting the separate allegations made against each in turn, had a vested interest in the general defence, i.e., that there was no affray apart from that which was created by police conduct, and to this general defence all counsel contributed. On the other hand, in the murder case of Campbell and Jones at the Old Bailey (this title is fictitious but the case is real) each defendant had a vested interest in placing the murder weapon, a knife, in the hands of the other and this of course was a cut-throat defence. Despite a united front in a given case it is open to co-defending counsel to first cross-examine the co-defendant before prosecution counsel gets to him. This opportunity can be used by co-defending counsel to clarify certain matters favourable to his own client or to present a united defence. For example, in the Lynch House affray case, one co-defendant Lennox Smith, had alleged that he had been kicked in the head by a police officer. The first co-defendant to give evidence was not able to give evidence to seeing that kick to Allen's head. It was necessary for

Allen's counsel to elicit in cross-examination, before prosecution counsel's turn came around, that persons standing between the witness's line of vision and Allen could well have obstructed sight of the kick. That done, prosecution counsel's guns, on this point at least, were well and truly spiked in advance.

There are cases, however, where co-defendants attack each other, i.e. try to shift the blame on to the shoulders of another defendant. Where this happens, a dog-eat-dog situation rapidly develops. In this situation no holds are barred and where a co-defendant gives evidence to the effect of undermining another defendant's defence then a dogfight breaks out with each defendant attacking the others' criminal record, if any. One of the most damaging speeches heard in a court of law was the verbal lashing meted out (quite properly) by Cardiff barrister Martin Everest when co-defending two punks charged with the same affray as the man they allegedly attacked. Co-defending counsel operates under none of the restraints that inhibit prosecution counsel. Co-defending counsel usually confer before a case to establish what degree of support or contradiction exists between parties and usually counsel on both sides are reasonbly frank about these matters; others are less so and one should not go into a co-defending situation with illusions. Unfortunately, where different individuals are charged with matters arising out of the same set of facts, then separate trials are hardly ever granted unless the trial judge can be satisfied that the prejudicial effect so greatly outweighs the probative value to make fair trial of any one defendant impossible.

There are unpleasant situations in which the prosecution and some co-defendants are so closely allied against one defendant as to make the combined effect absolutely staggering but again this is an occupational hazard that one has to live with. Co-defending counsel's line of attack may well be so radically removed from your own that any onlooker may easily get the impression that they are watching two separate trials. For example, there is the embarrassment that is inevitable when one defendant is mounting the most sweeping and comprehensive attack on the prosecution on grounds of fabrication of evidence while another co-defendant, sometimes as a matter of ultra-clever tactics, simply puts his challenges on grounds of honest mistake.

The prosecution nearly always benefits from such dogfights and most of the successful defences in multihanded trials have come where the prosecution has had to deal with a united defence. Defence counsel would do much better more often, if they cannot support a co-defence, at least not to join with the prosecution in attacking a co-defendant. Sometimes co-defending counsel get carried away in that they attack their co-defendants even when no obvious benefits could accrue but trial judges are unable effectively to intervene as between co-defending counsel. Hence the origin of the Chinese maxim: "With Co-defendants like these . . . who needs a prosecutor?"

Chapter Nineteen

Cases which are Wholly or Partly Based on Identification

The problem of cases involving the vexed question of identification is still receiving much attention from the judiciary and, in such cases, where identification is perhaps the sole issue, cross-examination must be fashioned rapier-like to the point. There are of course cases where the issue of identification is made easier for the prosecution by the existence of other supporting evidence. Where cross-examination as to the lighting conditions, speed and surprise of the events, the amount of time afforded to the witness all combine to make conviction highly dangerous. Judges of course must warn juries that it is dangerous to convict if the evidence of identification is unsupported by other evidence.

Such circumstances might arise as in the case of Leslie George Jones at Birmingham Crown Court where the alleged facts were that a number of black youths had attacked police officers late in the night after a blues party in Handsworth. The defendant Leslie George Jones was not arrested at the scene but, some few weeks later, he was sitting in his local police station when a police officer walked in and purported to identify him as one of those youths who had attacked police on the night in question.

That single identification by that solitary police officer was the only evidence against Jones made weeks after the event. Jones immediately denied the allegation and alleged frame-up in his defence at trial. That was the very narrow compass of trial.

In this sort of case involving a number of youths, fast movement, noise, violence, screams, darkness and limited opportunity for observation, there are certain questions which spring to mind as the obvious lines of cross-examination. The lighting from the street lamp was agreed as giving a "distorted effect." It was agreed that the police officer had never seen Jones before apart from the time which he claimed of the purported identification, there was violence by a number of persons and there was noise, screams and general confusion; fear and pandemonium, including visual confusion, were carefully painted in through cross-examination.

The identifying witness claimed to have identified three youths amongst those who had attacked him. It was necessary therefore to establish what time and visual opportunity was afforded him to make such identification.

The witness said that he was rolled up in a ball, curled up to protect himself from kicks and punches. He admitted to being frightened and said that his first thoughts were to protect himself from attack including the covering of his head and eyes with his hands. He claimed that there was one period of about three to four seconds when he lowered his hands from his head to call for police help over his personal radio. It was during this brief period of three to four seconds that he claimed to have seen the faces of three of the attacking youths well enough to identify them later.

The Court of Appeal has said that where a case is based substantially or wholly on identification of this kind the trial judge should give serious consideration to the stopping of the case. In this case, the judge left the decision to the jury – the jury acquitted. Birmingham police are well-known for employing some strange methods of identification and some at the Birmingham Bar are largely to blame for not attacking such methods strongly enough and some of the Birmingham judiciary for not ruling out such methods often enough.

It can be seen therefore that, where appropriate, cross-examination should deal with lighting, noise, movement, speed, confusion, opportunity for seeing faces and the delay between alleged sighting and purported identification. Identification in the dock of a magistrates court or in a police station when one is sitting alone are, needless to say, not ideal conditions allowing fair comparison with others of similar demeanour and general appearance.

Chapter Twenty

Submissions at the End of the Prosecution Case

At the end of the case for the prosecution comes the opportunity to make submissions of law to the trial judge in respect of the law and/or the quality of the evidence on the different charges.

All submissions msut be made within the straightjacket of law and upon the evidence as tested in cross-examination before the jury.

Counsel should be armed not only with his much-thumbed copy of Archbold but also with recent leading cases upon the subject. One need not bring up the entire arsenal of cases, there are usually one or two leading cases which cover all the ground. But submissions must be prepared so that counsel goes straight in without wasting too much judicial time. The shortest submission in a murder case that succeeded took no more than two minutes because all counsel concerned and the judge too realised the cross-examination had been so precise and unanswerable that the prosecution simply conceded that there was no case to go to the jury on murder or manslaughter (The Trial of Gary Huggins and the Thornton Heath 15). There should really be little confusion about the law or as to the geographical frontiers of the evidence; the only trick is to seek to fit the evidence within the legal ingredients necessary for the offence to be established and linked with the named defendant.

In some cases, the submission will be that there is NO CASE at all to go to the jury as where no witness places the defendant near or at the scene of the offence, i.e. there is no link of any kind.

The other submission might be that while the evidence discloses a lesser offence, e.g. actual bodily harm, there is not enough evidence on the greater offence, e.g. grievous bodily harm, because the medical evidence will not support the greater charge.

Submissions are simply a permutation of law and evidence and it is a taking-stock position so that no charges are left to the jury where there is no evidential foundation. In the case of Jefferson Smith at Cardiff Crown Court His Honour Judge Rutter QC withdrew six charges from the jury almost without calling upon defence counsel and with the immediate agreement of the prosecution. In the Higgins murder case, Treasury Counsel Roy Amlot simply did not suggest that such evidence existed.

Chapter Twenty One

Opening the Defence

At the beginning of every criminal trial Prosecution Counsel "opens" the case for the Prosecution. He identifies the defendants, lists the charges, deals with the relevant law and outlines the evidence upon which the prosecution will rely in order to prove its case against the defendant. Some opening speeches for the prosecution are absolutely deadly and certain masters of the art can almost substitute their opening words for hard evidence to the extent that these are the first words the jury hears in the case and the first chance the defence gets to intervene is that very first cross-examination of that very first witness. Defence counsel in the criminal trial very rarely employ an opening speech and this has largely fallen into disuse which, in my view, is a very great mistake.

The opening speech has to deal with the witness and the evidence which the defence will rely on. But defence counsel is not limited simply to dealing with the evidence which the defence will call. At this half-way stage, he can properly utilise this opportunity to make comment on the quality of the prosecution case. Some barristers prefer not to mount attack at this early stage and simply limit their speeches to the defence case since it is felt that mounting too early an attack on the prosecution case can make that later closing speech somewhat anti-climactic. It is a decision to be taken on the facts of each case but this opening speech, skilfully deployed, can much support that most precisely-balanced instrument, the presumption of innocence. Counsel will deal with this speech in his own way and in his own style but there are certain essential ingredients which could much assist to prepare the collective mind of the jury to be more open and receptive to the defence case.

One way of beginning such an address would be to emphasise to that jury that it is no part of the duty of defence counsel to attempt to deceive them into coming to a false conclusion. The jury should be addressed as seekers after Truth and should be urged most strongly to remember that the oath they took as jurors was to try the case not upon conjecture or speculation but "upon the evidence."

It is useful before one begins to outline the case for the defence to ask the rhetorical question: "What is the case against the defendant? What is the case the defence has to meet?" It is important to ask this question since, by the time the prosecution has closed its case, there will inevitably have been very many matters which would not have been disputed so that the areas of dispute have been narrowed down, e.g., in the case of Leslie George Jones, all the issues had been narrowed down purely and simply to the reliability or not of a single identification by a single police officer.

Once the question: "What is the case the defence has to meet?" is asked this then allows counsel for the defence to criticise, if he finds it relevant and timely, matters of contradiction and inconsistency in the prosecution case. Obviously, counsel will do well to reserve the launching of the main burden of his attack for his final closing speech but a few preliminary shots across the bows at this stage are never wasted. Juries look instinctively for the spirited and zestful and confident defence and do not respond well to timid defence speeches.

When counsel for the defence comes to that stage of his address of actually outlining the evidence he will rely on he has to be careful not to overstate his case. It is far better for the opening speech to be low-key in not raising a jury's expectations so that defence witnesses may heighten its effect in a three-dimensional way.

The other caution worthy of being exercised is that defence counsel should not outline the defence evidence in too great detail because more often than not defence witnesses do not live up to their proofs as given to defence solicitors not because of dishonesty but sometimes because of nervousness or absentmindedness.

Counsel's opening speech could well be used to narrow the issues, elicit a receptive state of mind from the jury and generally pave the way for calling of defence witnesses.

But, although one would advise in general a low-key pitch to such an opening speech, it all may depend on the very foundation of the defence and the content of earlier cross-examination: cross-examination in the classic murder case of Regina -v- Donat Smith did not allow for anything but a veritable mindblowing opening speech.

There is really, on the other hand, little scope for the opening speech in a trial which lasts over one or two days. But one can see the weapon more clearly if one considers that, in the Smith case, the prosecution case alone had lasted two whole months! At the end of two months of prosecution case there is then an absolute need to restore the balance even before the defence begins.

CHAPTER TWENTY TWO

Defendant's Right not to give Evidence

The defendant in the criminal trial has a legal entitlement to give evidence on his own behalf or to say nothing at all. This is his absolute right in law and it is important to stress that this right is not transferable to counsel but is a right which only the defendant can exercise. It is often said in the robing room that defence barristers who launch a massive attack on the prosecution and then do not "call" the defendant in evidence are guilty of some sort of professional impropriety but, of course, counsel for the defence cannot make up a defendant's mind for him on this point and counsel would be failing in his duty if he did not launch such attack on his written instructions so to do. Again, the defendant's right to give evidence or not is exercisable by him right up to the moment just before he chooses, if he does, to leave the dock and walk to the witness-box. No person can fetter this right in any way and no blame or criticism can attach to the defence barrister if the client, having ordered an Armageddon of cross-examination then, cowardly perhaps, even wisely some might say, does not enter the witness-box.

Of course, more often than not, the decision not to give evidence, even after the most fierce cross-examination, has been taken jointly well in advance after the most careful consultation between barrister, solicitors and counsel but the principle remains untouched. Of course, nearly always the decision not to give evidence is taken because the defendant has mounted such an attack on the prosecution that his own previous criminal record would be cross-examined upon if he gave evidence and the defence has to consider what may be the massively prejudicial effect of exposing such convictions to the jury.

The trial judge should really not be allowed to make any adverse comment whatsoever on the failure of the defendant to give evidence but some trial judges are too fond of making acidic and barbed references to such failure; remarks like, "Well, members of the jury, you must not hold it against him that he has chosen not to give evidence before you but you might think that, if he had, you might have gained some benefit from such assistance." It is submitted that judges should be stopped from making this kind of sarcastic reference although, of course, in many cases the absence of the defendant's evidence leaves a vacuum in which the prosecution case is uncontradicted by any sworn testimony.

However, the defendant is entitled to remain silent and, in effect, say to the prosecution: "You have brought these charges against me, you prove your case. I will exercise my right to stay silent. Let the jury see the quality of your evidence against me."

The burden of proving guilt begins and ends with the prosecution and that burden never shifts except, of course, on charges of living off the immoral earnings of a woman where different circumstances prevail. The prosecution must prove its case so that each and every one of the jury is satisfied and sure of guilt. For these reasons, before the defendant makes his decision as to whether or not to give evidence, certain questions fall for discussion between client and lawyers.

The first questions that have to be asked in conference with the defendant are:

1. What is the strength of the prosecution case?
2. How strong is the defence case?
3. Can the defence case get any better than it is at the end of the prosecution's?

More often than not the defence case cannot get any better in the sense that the prosecution case has been so much weakened by cross-examination that nothing further would be gained by calling any defence evidence.

In many cases, the defendant in the witness box turns out to be his own worst enemy and care should be taken to ensure that defendants are only advised to give evidence if the defence barrister feels that the defence case can be strengthened thereby. In some cases, there is just an absolute necessity for the defendant to give evidence which only he can deal with, e.g., in the case of a signed confession and here the choice is largely taken away by the circumstances of the case.

The decision not to give evidence has the advantage in that it forces the jury to concentrate on the prosecution case, contradictions, conflicts, warts and all. But this remains a brave choice and not lightly taken.

CHAPTER TWENTY THREE

The Defendant in the Witness Box

By the time the defendant takes to the witness-box the jury's appetite for his version of events will have been well and truly whetted in that, if the case has not been thrown out by the judge at end of the prosecution case it means not only that there is a case to go before the jury but that the defence version of events runs contrary to the prosecution's and the word on oath of the defendant, tested in cross-examination, can win or lose a case. And, of course, not being allowed to know how a jury's mind works, trying to gauge the impact of a defendant's evidence on a jury is largely guesswork since some harrowing stories do creep out of the jury room and some juries are influenced more by demeanour and appearances of sincerity rather than by the actual words of denial. But these matters are still capable of being put broadly in the sense that a defendant should not be let loose in the witness-box without some preparation.

It should be emphasised that some solicitors do not prepare the case fully and some leave out areas of information which counsel's brief should automatically contain, e.g., a full list of the defendant's previous criminal record. For this reason, it is most important for defence counsel first of all to master his client's proof, and where the sequence of instruction is wrong, to reorder its contents. Secondly, he must go through the proof carefully with his lay client in the presence of his instructing solicitors. Thirdly, he should cross-examine his client most thoroughly in conference and play Devil's Advocate to the hilt so that his client gets a full taste of prosecution-style cross-examination. If your client is telling the truth he should stand up well to it but if he starts jumping about in conference then you've got a problem on your hands.

Defendants should be told of the need to dress cleanly and smartly before a jury and they should be told of the need to answer simply and clearly without making long, rambling speeches in answer to a short question. They should be warned of areas of provocation which might ensue when the prosecution start to cross-examine. They should be told that, above all, they should listen carefully to the question asked and answer as simply as possible. Too many defendants, especially those whose long list of previous criminal convictions are before a jury, go into stupid and dishonest explanations of quite simple questions. Simplicity and brevity are the best assistants to the defendant in the witness box.

If his previous criminal convictions are going to be placed before the jury then it is better if these are first elicited by the defence and not sprung as a surprise on the jury by the prosecution. A defendant who "tells it all" about his previous convictions is more prepared psychologically, and so is the jury, to meet questions about his murky past. That done, defence counsel should then take his client slowly, there is absolutely no need to hurry, through his own story. When that story is finished, defence counsel then sits down and awaits cross-examination by the prosecution.

Ideally, it is better for the defence never having to interrupt prosecution counsel on his feet. Ideally, save any matters for the end when you can yourself re-examine your own client to put matters of clarification arising from cross-examination. It is only if prosecution counsel is not allowing your client to make full answer or is in some way advancing half-truths that you should interrupt. Ideally, let your client stand on his own feet. It is his defence, not yours.

When the time comes for re-examination, again ideally, it is best left alone, if you can. The truthful client will need no extra help from you. But if, and only if, you feel that you must, then ask the extra few final questions only for clarification. And do not forget to invite the trial judge to say whether he or she has any further questions before you return your client to the dock. A defendant who has been superb in the witness-box will have written your closing speech for you and a client who has been devastated will have made your life more difficult and closing speeches written in the imagination can all be torn up after the defendant has given evidence.

:

CHAPTER TWENTY FOUR

Witnesses for the Defence

In a case where contradiction and confrontation of the prosecution case is the name of the game, almost never call witnesses with previous criminal convictions for dishonesty. That said, it should stand to reason that your instructing solicitors have investigated the background of their witnesses. This area of omission by solicitors can be a minefield for defence counsel since, although you can speak to your client in conference, you are not allowed to speak to witnesses and you are left totally at the mercy of your solicitors. You should insist that solicitors double-check witnesses on this point.

Witnesses called by the defence are called, by definition, to support some material aspect of the defence case, e.g., witnesses of alibi who will say that the defendant was in another place at the material time. It also follows that such witnesses are called to give testimony consistent with the defendant's version of events and a lazily-taken proof can prove lethal. For example, in a case of affray, apart from solicitors asking the witness to state what the witness saw of other people attacking or fighting it is absolutely crucial to mount a prosecution-style interrogation of the witness to elicit matters potentially detrimental to the defence. The defendant's version is the blueprint to which you must work and witnesses who do not support this blueprint must not be called.

Usually, the reason why defence witnesses differ from the defendant or from other defence witnesses is not because they are lying witnesses but because of faulty recollection. Sometimes witnesses are seen much too late after events by solicitors, and, by that late hour, their memory has faded or become inexact. The other reason for inconsistency may be because solicitors have omitted to put to the witness crucial matters for clarification or verification.

Since the function of defence witnesses is to give a coherent, logical, honest and full account of events consistent with the defendant's version, any defence counsel who lets loose witnesses who contradict the defence case wants his head examined. You are not instructed to give hostages to Fortune.

Many a time have defences been lost by enthusiastic witnesses giving rich, varied and even colourful accounts that are at complete variance with the defence case and here it cannot be too strongly emphasised that a criminal case is often lost or won because of lazy or incompetent preparation by defence solicitors. This area of defence witnesses is one of the crucial areas in the criminal trial.

CHAPTER TWENTY FIVE

Closing Speech by Defence Counsel

Before your Final Speech you will have listened to the Closing Speech of Counsel for the Prosecution and you will have made full notes of such arguments advanced by him which, in your view, should be attacked as inconsistent with the evidence in the case. Indeed, the first vibrant words to fall from your lips should nearly always be words of attack on what has just fallen from your learned friend.

Defence Counsel should note with care the contents of his opponent's closing speech. It is your duty to watch for any references which are not borne out by the evidence or are logical inferences which can be drawn from it. The closing speech by prosecution counsel will inevitably offer much scope and material for comment by the defence and the time for such comment is when you rise to your feet for your own closing speech. But, by and large, by this time, the trial is all over bar the shouting and unless the quality of the prosecution evidence has been poor or there has been radical departure in the form of unexpected and favourable defence evidence, your final speeches tend to be more summary than persuasion.

But, in a proper case, defence counsel's speech to the jury can sometimes be the pièce de résistance and the first lesson is that defence counsel must never make the mistake of attuning his own speech to the style, attack and temperature of the prosecution's. Most prosecution speeches are very dull anyway and it is usually nothing short of professional death to emulate the graveyard stances and the droning tones of prosecution counsel. The wavelength of closing speech for the defence must aim for style, attack, verve and conviction in the honesty of the defence case.

The Closing Speech is the time for marshalling the facts of the defence in a totally convincing way. The facts of the case MUST, by this time, have been totally mastered by Defence Counsel and this is no time for fumbling through papers or getting facts or figures wrong. This speech must be most carefully prepared but, where the evidence in the case has changed unexpectedly, then you have to trim your sails accordingly.

For example, in the Trial of the Cricklewood 12, Dennis Bovell (yes, the great musician himself), Royfield Brown and Oliver Smith were retried (as the remaining nine defendants had been acquitted in the first trial) before His Honour Judge Abdela QC and the learned judge had to direct the jury on the laws relating to identification.

Oliver Smith was acquitted but Bovell and Brown were convicted and sentenced to terms of imprisonment after Judge Abdela's direction to the jury. The Court of Appeal, in the person of Lord Justice Lawton, blasted Judge Abdela's summing-up as "the total converse of what a trial judge should do" and Brown and Bovell were freed. It is important therefore to make careful note of the summing-up of what the trial judge says since, if there be a misdirection in law, you will have to advise on the basis of your own notes whether there can be grounds of appeal against such misdirection of law. You should have prepared your law thoroughly by this time and you may advance – but simply and clearly – what, in your view, the legal ingredients of the offences charged are; and counsel for the defence who can deal with the law with simplicity and lucidity is worth his weight in gold, if not Legal Aid!

The first line of attack of the closing speech should be: "What is the evidence of the Prosecution?"

Prosecution evidence can be contradicted, confused, discredited, and generally destroyed in some cases and yet the judge leaves the case to the jury. In the Trial of the Bristol Riots this is what happened and yet the case was left to the jury and closing speeches were almost extravagant and unnecessary after the havoc wreaked on the helpless Director of Public Prosecutions.

This is the last word that the jury will hear from defence counsel addressing himself to the totality of the case and this final speech must be well prepared. The form of preparation differs from barrister to barrister but a barrister who reads out every single word will not make a good speech. Good speeches should be listed point by point by point and a good barrister will know how to expand that single point into an eloquent paragraph of words. Simply go through the facts of the case as you see them and list them as points. Then re-list them in the order in which you wish to take them. Then use this as your list of points to be made.

Some Counsel leave the law to the end of the speech, some prefer dealing with the law at the beginning, some intersperse law with the facts. I found from many years experience that the law is best dealt with slowly and thoroughly at the beginning of one's final speech, largely because law tends to be a bit antiseptic to the lay listener but, more importantly, because the law is the legal framework for the jury's consideration of the facts and best give them the law first before the facts.

There are quite a number of fundamental points that need to be made well into the final speech before one turns to the facts and the first of these is the Burden of Proof or, alternatively phrased, the Presumption of Innocence. The jury need to have clearly hammered home to them this very fundamental starting point in that they must be made to be totally aware that that burden never shifts and always stays with the prosecution. Do not leave this to the judge - some simply skate over this very essential foundation stone and you would do best not to ignore or trifle with it. Once you have made the Burden of Proof clear then move over the the Standard of Proof.

The jury should, once again, be made clear that the standard in a criminal trial is one of high satisfaction and not one on the balance of probabilities. This high level of satisfaction must apply to all crucial points that the prosecution must prove; if defences like self-defence are raised then, again, the jury must be told that it is for the prosecution to satisfy them that self-defence does not apply, not for the defence to prove that it does.

The third fundamental point to make is that a jury's deliberations must be "according to the evidence" and not upon conjecture or speculation and certainly it must never be on prejudice. This last word, prejudice, will offer Counsel serious difficulties in a case where your client's character involving previous similar convictions have been laid before the jury and, if your client is charged with burglary, the fact that he has four or five previous convictions for burglary is difficult to shake off and sometimes it is one hell of a job getting a jury not to utilise such previous record to found a disbelief of your defence and the conviction of your client.

The other rather delicate matter is that juries should be reminded but in guarded and civil tones, if you wish to stay in practice, that judicial guidance on inferences of the evidence should be firmly rejected by juries - it is their function to try your client not the judge's and you have to get on with building that psychological brickwall between the minds of the jury and that wise old owl up there!

The law in the criminal case is nearly always easy and simple to state and judges in the criminal courts nearly always get it right. Nevertheless, it is your duty to review the law and to state it comprehensively in your closing speech. Don't just do it once – do it at the beginning of your speech and repeat it at the end as you take the jury through the indictment.

Counsel's closing speech will have been shaped, if not reshaped, by the evidence called by the defence and many a good speech is torn up after defence witnesses have savaged their own defence. Many a final speech involves the trimming of a good many sails after the defendant has given evidence and you may find that a large chunk of your final speech has to be introduced spontaneously to do with some blunder or damage that your client has introduced. If this happens then your duty is to be realistic and honest with the jury. Juries are not blind and they have the collective perception of twelve pairs of eyes and ears. If there is a weak point in your case, face up to it squarely and don't try building bricks out of straw – you may have to cut your losses to get your client off attempted murder knowing full well that he is going down for wounding.

Above all, your final speech must be founded soundly on the evidence that has been given and best deal with matters chronologically. Wherever possible, deal with matters of common ground first and go into disputed territory later. Deal with weak points first and strong points later.

If you have prepared your speech as above then the rest is stance, delivery and style. Stand up, speak up and shut up! Please do not slouch nor twiddle your fingers. Fact the jury face on and look them full in the face. Do NOT look at a point above the jurybox – look at every juror two by two and three by three and keep looking them squarely in the eyes. Your voice much be bold, loud and clear but not a monotonous drone. Remember inflexions, nuances, humour, charm as the actor remembers on stage. The final speech is a lot of theatre and barristers for the defence must, above all, speak up with some gusto.

Accents should be lost if they are difficult to comprehend as soon as possible after joining the Bar since the jury must not miss a single word that you say and every word must count. Clarity and precision every time.

Properly prepared and delivered this final speech can be a thing of poetry and beauty and splendid craftsmanship. At the end of the day, the purpose of your speech is to secure acquittal for your client and your cloth must be cut accordingly. Do not cut short your speech because the judge is throwing tantrums or making faces. Do not withdraw a word or phrase of it because of judicial displeasure – it is your speech not the judge's and it is your client's neck on the block, not the judge's. 'Prepare well and stick to your guns.' Nor should you rush your speech or cut it short because you think the jury is not listening to you – you have a duty to your client and you must never shrink from it.

The above does not mean that your speech must be of too great a length. In the Bristol Riots counsel had to address the jury for two and a half days but that was deliberate strategy in placing the evidence at some length before the jury (before the judge got it!) but *the classic closing* speech, in my view, was in 1970 in the Trial of the Metro Four – it lasted forty-five minutes and secured twenty-four verdicts of Not Guilty.

CHAPTER TWENTY SIX

Blacks At The Bar

No reference to practising in the British criminal courts would be complete without specific reference to the 268 black barristers practising at the English Bar. The Bar, effectively operating as Britain's smallest profession with a maximum of about 6,000 practitioners in London out of which barely 1,000 can be said to be practising exclusively in the criminal courts, thus has a 25% black representation among the ranks of the criminal Bar and therefore it is important to examine the circumstances which attend their professional presence in England's most conservative profession.

Reference to Britain's black practitioners is important for two reasons. The first is that their continuing treatment by a profession dedicated to the dispensing of justice without bias is worthy of public rebuke and the second reason is that black lawyers in the criminal courts have totally revolutionised the approach of white defence lawyers in political cases.

One needs to view the coming of black legal practitioners in its historical context and for that we must go back to the late 1960's. At that time the only Chambers in the entire Inns of Court who took blacks were the chambers of the late Sir Dingle Foot QC, a man, like many others, with a New Commonwealth practice but unlike the others who had exploited and profited from black Privy Council work (even flying out like legal missionaries to bring 'legal civilisation' to their African, Asian and Caribbean brothers), Foot was the only one who could stomach a black man in his chambers. True, that first black man came in the celebrated form of the legendary Learie Constantine but his chambers stayed consistent on the race issue. Others proved to be non-racist while they enjoyed black hospitality in Africa but proved racist on their return to the Inner Temple. Blacks were consistently refused even pupillages at the Bar and many brilliant black barristers were lost to the Civil Service or were forced to leave England.

There were, however, some blacks who insisted on practising and names like Ashraf Bashiri, Lawrence St. Ville, George Davis and Mavis Gibson formed the first black set at 15 Old Square in Lincoln's Inn. Lincoln's Inn has always been more than hospitable to black practitioners.

Racism at the Bar stayed rampant despite my public speeches and newspaper articles and the official response was to bring disciplinary proceedings against those who spoke out (see Barrister On Trial, 1980.)

More blacks set up after being refused places and the hypocrisy of the profession was such that, after refusing the blacks, the very same white Heads of Chambers who had refused them places wrung their hands and beat their breasts and stated how much they regretted the formation af "all black" chambers! The position now is that all the black Heads of Chambers have allowed themselves to be persuaded that all-black chambers are bad (while all stay silent about the dozens of all-white chambers who still will not take on blacks!). I maintain that among the young blacks names like Harry Narayan, Ovais Kadri, Mirza Rashid, William Panton, Delano Bart, Maria Fernandes, Mike Magloire, Harjit Grewal, Eddie Cofie, Ita Marshall, Jeffrey Yearwood and others are more than a match for their English counterparts and one hopes that the Lord Chancellor's office and the prosecuting solicitors will now radically reappraise their attitudes to black practitioners.

The Bar moved into token acknowledgement of its own racism after a community conference at Loughborough University, made up of 120 of the national black leadership, called on the Commission for Racial Equality to formally investigate the profession and after my Bar Council trial in 1980 when the black grassroots invaded Gray's Inn and broke down doors.

After that the Bar decided to set up a Working Party on Race Relations. But there is still room for improvement.

First of all, some blacks are still being refused places in Chambers while well-meaning black heads like John Roberts and Brenton Mitchell are doing their best to create multi-racial sets. Secondly, solicitors for the Commissioner of the Metropolitan Police in London, and the Chief Constables outside, refuse to allow too many black barristers to prosecute. Thus, at a stroke, half the work at the criminal bar is denied to the majority of black practitioners. The situation has changed slightly in the past three years in that one or two blacks are being allowed to prosecute.

Thirdly, black practitioners are still being refused appointments to the magistracy and to the Judiciary. Out of some 546 Recorders in the Crown Courts, at the time of writing, not one is black, although there are now a handful of Assistant Recorders. There is one single solitary black judge, His Honour Judge Mota Singh. There is one single full-time stipendiary magistrate, Mr. Anura Cooray. There is no black Queen's Counsel.

I state the above in one final effort to persuade those in authority to make appointment of blacks at all levels. Black defendants are not that lacking in perception in that the black community can see that the black practitioner is always seen in a defending role and the judges are hardly ever black. A just society must reflect those of all races at all levels. To exclude people is to leave them out on the streets where violence in the form of riots is their only resort. Despite the enlightening lead given by distinguished voices like Lord Scarman the British legal profession is proving slow to budge from its entrenched position.

A few final words to my brothers and sisters at the Bar. One cannot fight a holy war with both hands tied behind one's back. Incompetence is not the best ally in the fight and unprofessional practices like touting for work, taking money direct from clients and seeing clients without solicitors will not do. To hold yourself out as a practitioner to a man facing loss of liberty, to his family in distress, to take money off the poor and weak, and then not to be competent in court is the most disgraceful thing that you can do. Either straighten up or abandon a profession which cannot afford such practitioners. If these words have to be said then I am quite happy to be the one to say it. I hope these words are taken with the sincerity with which they are employed. We cannot fight against racial discrimination while we continue to provide living justification upon which discrimination can be rationalised. Our duty is to be worthy of all the remedies and rectifications for which I have argued in this chapter.

No record of the black bar would be complete without recording their many great victories in cases beginning with the Metro Four in 1970, through stirring cases like the Stockwell 10, the Islington 18, the Cricklewood 12, the Thornton Heath 15 and, more recently their participation in the Bradford 12. It is not only that they have won but that they have actually changed the style of defence advocacy at the English Bar. Where barristers once winced before putting harsh allegations to police officers the black bar has pioneered the pointblank style of attack in criminal cases and other barristers have been forced to change their own styles to meet the volatility and vividness of black defence counsel.

The black bar, with all its disadvantages and obstacles, has made its contributions to a just society and all it now needs is for the Bar of England and Wales to recognise their contribution by appropriate promotion and appointments. To this end, one congratulates the Lord Chancellor's office on the appointment of John Roberts and Len Woodley as Assistant Recorders and hope that more will follow.

Conclusion to Part I

I have tried in the preceding chapters to give some guidance not only to the young practitioner but also to the ordinary citizen as to the defence aspect of the criminal trial.

Advocates, of course, are born not made and the ability to think quickly on one's feet is inherent, almost instinctive and, in some people, quite incapable of cultivation.

But, given moderate intelligence and lots of sweat, there can be massive improvement in the ranks of defence counsel presently practising at the Bar of England and Wales.

The present state of some incompetence arises largely because the Bar has, until recently, never taken the proper training of advocates as a serious responsibility. Consequently, the standards are less than they should be and a few people have gone to prison because of the incompetence of their defence barristers. Incompetence takes many forms and one form of incompetence is the refusal by some defence counsel to confront corrupt police and a sometimes biased judge or magistrate. The reluctance has remained despite harrowing stories told by the citizen client of experiences at the hands of the police.

I take the view that the police, for obvious reasons, can look after themselves, contemporaneous notes and all and my personal experience has been that police officers, generally speaking, hold no personal grudges against defence lawyers who merely put their clients' instructions. In this context, it is worth stating that, while certain police officers are corrupt and do tell lies, the majority of the police officers who give evidence day-in and day-out in our criminal courts are themselves quite decent, family men with the same preoccupations with family and children and balancing their home budgets that we all experience. They are in the force to do a professional job and so are we and one professional should not be hostile to another; there should be mutual respect of each other's position and we should both do our jobs honestly and efficiently.

But, if the client gives certain clear instructions then the police forces must understand that we are only advocates, we are not judge and jury; it is their task to prosecute, it is ours to defend.

It follows therefore that defence counsel up and down the country should be more fearless in the pursuit of their clients' defences and police authorities should be less hostile to defence barristers.

I hold no brief for corrupt lawyers, and there are certainly some of those about, but, barring these rotten apples, as in the police forces, there are many decent, hardworking people about and this resentment of the vigorous defender should be replaced by respect and tolerance of the professional's high duty to his lay client.

Upon the question of competence Pupilmasters should not extend Certificates of Competence to pupils who are clearly not well-equipped for the profession. The Bar should ensure that only pupils who can muster Certificates of Competence from Pupilmaster and Head of Chambers (where he did his pupillage) are awarded Practising Certificates and such Certificates of Competence should only be awarded after the most careful scrutiny of the aspirant's performance over a period of his year's pupillage.

Unless the Bar adopts this proposal, matters will continue as before where some barristers without real ability go through formal pupillages and emerge into practice without any real ability. If this trend continues the public will continue to pay dearly with some innocent men being convicted and the Bar must continue to move to improve standards at the defence Bar.

It may be that pupillages can be extended to include a given number of attendances upon judges and upon a minimum number of important cases with the duty of the pupil making notes up for inspection by a panel of practising barristers. Whichever method is employed, there is clear need to improve standards and I have no hesitation in making this call.

I hope that this little book helps at least to provoke thought and discussion about the criminal trial. The criminal trial remains one of the most crucial areas of human endeavour and the defence lawyer one of the high architects of that endeavour.

The public interest demands a constant review and reappraisal of the standards of commitment and competence of defence lawyers everywhere and the interests of the prisoner awaiting trial is very much the interest of all who prize the need for all to be presumed innocent until, after proper defence work, he be found guilty upon clear evidence. But it must be a message of "clients first, lawyers second" – only in this way can we serve the public.

It is my fervent desire to see the coming of a new breed of defence lawyers armed with fluency, style and vigour to the terror of suspect prosecutions. To this aspiration I would commend the attention of the undergraduates in our law schools all over. The call I make, therefore, is a call to the ranks of defenders of the poor, the oppressed and the exploited. The rich and the powerful can, and will, take care of themselves!

Will you join me in the Fight?

Rudy Narayan,
67 Chancery Lane,
London, WC2   May, 1985

IN PREPARATION

Rudy Narayan's "Without Prejudice" (the book of forthcoming BBC Television series).

Editor's Addendum

Rudy Narayan has been described by no less an authority than the eminent Law Lord, Lord Scarman, who presided over the Brixton Inquiry, as "one of the best cross-examiners in the Commonwealth". He has written the preceding chapters of this book and I have included extracts from his cross-examination of Phillip Cox QC at Narayan's public trial before the Bar Council in April 1980 and extracts from Narayan's cross-examination of witnesses at the Scarman Inquiry into the Brixton Riots in 1981, in order to illustrate the art of cross-examination so vividly described by him in the preceding part of the book.

Some of these extracts from his cross-examination have been given wide publicity in the TV and News Media and his speech to the 1980 tribunal was distributed at his Press Conference in 1980 and published by Hansib Pubishing (see *Barrister on Trial*) but as they are classic gems of the art of cross-examination and his genius of advocacy they deserve to be reproduced in this book.

Arif Ali, Editor-in-Chief, Justice Books, London.

Part II

Narayan's Cross-Examination of Phillip Cox QC
– Bar Council Trial, 1980

PART II

Excerpts from Narayan's Cross-Examination of Phillip Cox QC before the Disciplinary Tribunal of the Senate, April 1980.

As stated elsewhere in this book, cross-examination has many purposes and the excerpts from Rudy's own cross-examination of Philip Cox QC and later Narayan's cross-examination before the Scarman Inquiry into the Brixton Riots may offer vivid illustration of the technique.

In the cross-examination of Cox QC before press and public, it was important to demonstrate that both Bar and Law Society in Birmingham and the Bar Council in London were behind the prosecution against Narayan and his second question to Cox QC unleashes the dogs of war immediately. You will notice the phrasing of the first five questions being tailored on the "high duty" aspect of the witness's status. Note the way in which "background" is laid swiftly before press and public. Note the "sequence" of events put in cross-examination leading up to the kernel of the charges – the demolition of Cox QC as a witness was accomplished long before the last nine questions which sealed off all exits for the Bar Council's Henry Pownall QC.

Arif Ali

Cross-examination by Rudy Narayan

Q. Mr Cox, as one of Her Majesty's Counsel were you until recently leader of the Midland Circuit?

A. I was, yes.

Q. First of all, as one of Her Majesty's Counsel, do you have a very high duty to ensure that the legal profession acts in the interest of the public?

A. Certainly.

Q. As one of Her Majesty's Queen's Counsel do you have a duty to ensure that you are not prompted into actions by other persons outside the profession?

A. (Pause).

Q. May I re-phrase the question?

A. Yes. I am sorry, I do not really quite understand the question.

Q. As Queen's Counsel and as leader of the Midland Circuit, do you have a high duty to exercise your judgement independently of any other persuasion?

A. Certainly, yes, I must act upon my own judgement.

Q. One of the members of those chambers in Birmingham where your name is is a Mr. Richard Penn?

A. Yes.

Q. Do you know him?

A. He is now Head of those Chambers.

Q. Yes.

A. Yes, I know him well.

Q. Did you know that Mr Richard Penn stated in open court about Mr. Ashraf Bashiri, an Asian barrister, that "All Asian barristers are rogues"?

A. No.

Q. Did you know that?

A. As I heard that that had been said by Mr. Penn at some time, as I heard it, in a robing room somewhere on the Circuit.

Q. Did you know that I complained to the Bar Council against you for Richard Penn stating in public that all Asian barristers are rogues?

A. I am afraid I have no correspondence about this; I do not think I ever received correspondence.

Q. Never mind correspondence.

A. I think at some stage I heard someone had suggested, and I am not aware who, that I in some way had some sort of responsibility for what Mr Richard Penn said in my absence.

Q. Yes. Do you accept that those words were the subject of written complaint to the Bar Council; all Asian barristers are rogues?

A. I know that a complaint was made to the Bar Council about Mr. Penn's conduct.

THE CHAIRMAN: Mr Narayan, could you tell me what this had got to do with the charges? At the moment I have looked at the two letters and I have compated them with the charges. It appears to me that the charges are within a very narrow compass.

NARAYAN: This witness's credibility and honesty is about to be attacked.

THE CHAIRMAN: On what basis?

NARAYAN: I will put it in two questions. (To the witness): Do you find the words "All Asian barristers are rogues" offensive?

A. Yes.

Q. Have you, as leader of the Circuit, taken action against Richard Penn for saying all Asian barristers are rogues?

A. No.

Q. Why not?

A. Because no complaint has ever been made to me.

Q. Once you became aware that a member of the Chambers in the Circuit over which you are leader has allegedly made racist remarks of that nature, are you not under a duty to enquire?

A. The first I heard about this, Mr Narayan, was that a complaint had been made to the Professional Conduct Committee about Mr Penn's conduct. It is not my duty, Mr Narayan, as leader of the Circuit to enquire into a complaint which has been made to the Professional Conduct Committee.

Q. Let us put it this way. You know nothing was done by the Bar Council over those racialist remarks.

A. I do know what the Bar Council did. I am not a member of the Professional Conduct Committee, but I saw certain correspondence.

Q. Leaving aside what the Bar Council may do against Mr Penn for those remarks, do you accept, as leader of the Midland Circuit, the least you should do is drag Penn in and rap his knuckles for that kind of behaviour?

A. No, it depends whether it was true.

Q. You do not believe it was true?

A. I do not know whether it was true.

Q. You, of course, were the man who complained against me writing that letter and sending a copy to the press.

A. Yes. I received a letter from the Vice-President of the Birmingham Law Society enclosing a copy of the letter that you had sent to him and, if my memory serves me right, I was told a copy of the letter you had sent to the President or the Vice-President of the Birmingham Law Society had been sent to the press. When I read the letter I thought it my duty to draw the matter to the attention of the Professional Conduct Committee.

Q. What I am asking you is this. If you moved to complain about my letter to the press, which we have heard about, why have you not moved against white barrister Penn who says all Asian barristers are rogues?

A. Because no complaint has ever been drawn to my attention in relation to Mr Penn's conduct. I cannot act, Mr Narayan, in any respect in this sort of matter without some sort of complaint being made to me.

NARAYAN: I will re-phrase it. (To the Witness): Do you today, as you sit here now, condemn all racial remarks by members of the Bar against each other?

A. Certainly. I have never been a racialist. I do not know whether you know, Mr Narayan, but when I was Head in Chambers in Birmingham, I think I was the first Head of Chambers in Birmingham ever to accept an application for a pupillage by a black barrister into my chambers.

Q. Then you threw him out.

A. I did not.

Q. Charles Noel.

A. Mr Noel did a pupillage in my chambers and then I took Silk. What happened to Mr Noel after that was not in my control.

Q. You did not care.

A. Of course I cared! I am very concerned about harmonious relation between the races.

Q.When you ...

A. May I finish my answer. It is of the utmost importance that barristers of the English Bar, whatever their colour, work harmoniously together. There is room for everyone at the English Bar provided they obey the rules.

Q. When you were leader of the Midland Circuit do you remember the black barrister, Charles Noel, complaining he was not being given work?

A. Certainly.

Q. Do you remember that the matter was aired at a meeting of the Midland Circuit at which you presided?

A. Whether I was leader at the time or whether it was before I was leader I do not know, but I do remember a meeting in the library at the Victoria Law Courts in Birmingham, but if you will forgive me, I think it was before I became leader.

Q. At any rate Noel was then complaining of discrimination.

A. Mr. Charles Noel, so far as I remember, was not complaining of that, he was complaining that the Prosecuting Solicitor in Birmingham was not sending him briefs.

Q. That is right. Do you remember that the Prosecution Solicitor was invited to that meeting to say it was not because he was black but it was becaue he was incompetent?

A. I am sorry, I cannot remember that. It is many years ago now; I think it was probably about six years ago.

Q. Do you remember Mr. Emrys Morgan, the Prosecuting Solicitor, being invited physically to address a meeting of barristers in your presence and hearing?

A. Whether Mr Emrys Morgan did that I am afraid I cannot

remember. Mr Emrys Morgan would not be at a meeting of the Midland and Oxford Circuit.

Q. That is why I asked you. It was extraordinary if he was, was it not?

A. Whether he was or not I cannot remember.

Q. Do you remember the reason advanced against Mr. Noel's complaint then was that it was not because he was black, it was because he was incompetent?

A. I do not remember that. I can remember it being suggested at some time that the Prosecuting Solicitor, whether it was the Prosecuting Solicitor himself or someone speaking on his behalf or a letter being read out I cannot remember, what I do remember was it was made plain by the Prosecuting Solicitor that he, as Prosecuting Solicitor, had the right to choose counsel to prosecute and that he was not, as I remember, going to be dictated to by anyone as to whom he should choose.

Q. Do you accept this proposition, that a citizen is entitled to freedom of choice of counsel?

A. Certainly.

Q. Do you accept this further proposition, that a solicitor who obstructs a citizen in the exercise of that right is acting unprofessionally?

A. Yes. If a lay client wishes to have a particular barrister then, provided his solicitor is appraised of that knowledge and provided the solicitor is free to advise his client as to the wisdom of his choice, certainly the lay client is entitled to the barrister of his choice.

NARAYAN (To the Witness): Do you accept if a barrister of experience and distinction who defended and got acquittals in murder cases all over England is asked for, by name, of a solicitor and that solicitor says "No way, I am going to send Phillip Cox, QC instead" do you accept that the solicitor is acting unprofessionally?

A. If the lay client made the particular matter clear, certainly.

Q. This is my question and I thought I had got a clear "yes" from you. If a client says "I am charged with murder and I want barrister X" and barrister X is known as a barrister of much experience in the criminal courts and the solicitor refuses that client's instructions and says "No way", is that unprofessional?

A. Yes, other things being equal. When I say it is unprofessional, of course I am not the arbiter of professional conduct; all I can do is give my opinion as to what is professional and unprofessional conduct.

Q. You are giving your opinion as one of Her Majesty's Counsel?

A. Certainly, yes.

Q. As a senior member of the Bar, regardless of race or colour, if you were consistently being denied this right by solicitors in Birmingham, is that a matter of public interest?

A. Certainly it is.

Q. If you found that they were being denied this right in this way at the expense of black lawyers to the gain of white lawyers, is that a matter of public interest?

A. Yes.

Q. Would you agree with this: if solicitors in Birmingham have been consistently refusing to instruct black barristers and sending him to white, it would be the action of a gentleman on the part of the white barrister to refuse to take part in such an operation.

A. Yes, if one knew about it. If I knew that I was about to receive a brief because the solicitor was sending it to me in defiance of his client's instructions, I should refuse it.

Q. That is right. Incidentally, you and I know you sat on a Tribunal that suspended me in 1974.

A. That is some time ago. I cannot remember how long it was; time flies, Mr Narayan.

Q. The party concerned, a murder case, you remember, where the client got off, but I got six months at your hands. Did you know that?

A. No, I did not know anything about the case.

Q. You had a bundle of papers about my exchanges with the judge.

A. I had the transcript.

Q. It was a murder case where the client got off, but you gave me six months, is that not right?

A. Forgive me, I was not concerned with the trial, I was concerned, as I understood it on that Tribunal, with a complaint by Mr. Justice Ashworth about your conduct. We did not have a full transcript of the trial.

Q. We will leave that. Tell me this, as one of Her Majesty's Queen's Counsel, are you in the habit of allowing solicitors to phone you at home over professional matters?

A. Very rarely.

Q. Further to that, as one of Her Majesty's Queen's Counsel, are you in the habit of encouraging solicitors to write "Dear Phillip" and send letters to your home address?

A. I never encourage them.

Q. Before you complained against me, you received two secret letters from George Jonas addressed "Dear Phillip" to your home address, is that not true?

A. I will look at my file.

Q. I will show you the originals.

A. I prefer to look at my file.

Q. I will show you the originals.

THE WITNESS: Yes, I have a letter here dated the 28th September, 1978 addressed to me at my home address. I have another letter dated the 4th October, 1978.

THE CHAIRMAN: These are two letters from Mr Jonas?

A. Yes, both from Mr. Jonas. I have known Mr. Jonas since about 1950.

THE RESPONDENT: They were not letters from Mr. Jonas, they were letters from George, were they not? "Dear Phillip" signed "George"?

A. Yes.

Q. Do you accept this as one of Her Majesty's Queen's Counsel, that the Bar is a separate profession to the Law Society?

A. It is separate in the sense it is a different branch of the profession.

Q. You gave evidence partly to the Royal Commission saying that they should stay separate.

A. I did not actually give evidence, but I took part in the meeting. I have always believed ...

Q. That they should be separate.

A. That is in the interest of the public they should be separate.

Q. You know one of the fundamental principles of the practice of the Bar is that members of the Bar should not consort with solicitors with intent to private gain.

A. Certainly.

NARAYAN: I just want to put to this Queen's Counsel letters written to him "Dear Phillip" at his private home address signed "George".

THE CHAIRMAN: He has produced them.

NARAYAN: (To the Witness): Let me ask you about my first letter dated the 25th September.

A. This is your letter addressed to the President of the Birmingham Law Society, is it?

Q. That is right.

A. Yes, I have got a photostat copy.

Q. Before I ask you that, you knew, by the time I wrote that letter, that I had set up an annexe in Birmingham because we had correspondence?

A. Yes, I had correspondence from you. I had invited you to make application to become a member of the Midland and Oxford Circuit.

Q. That is right, and when I did not reply to the letters inviting me to join the Circuit your Junior, Elisabeth Fisher, on the 11th September wrote to me saying you were getting concerned.

A. Yes.

Q. That is 14 days before my letter of the 25th.

A. Yes.

Q. Did it reach your ears that as a result of my setting up an annexe in Birmingham black people were sacking white barristers in Birmingham?

A. No, no complaint was ever made to me.

Q. Not a complaint, did it reach your ears?

A. I am afraid it did not.

Q. Did you know that in the interest of justice certain white barristers were being sacked by black clients in Birmingham?

THE CHAIRMAN: Did you say that that was the result of your setting up an annexe?

NARAYAN: No, I am not saying as a result of but following.

THE CHAIRMAN: When you say "sacking" I understand you to mean not employing rather than dismissing in the middle of a case, am I right?

NARAYAN: No, sacking in open court.

THE CHAIRMAN: Sacking in open court?

NARAYAN: Yes.

THE WITNESS: No, I am afraid I did not hear that.

NARAYAN: I want to ask you about black people's cases in Birmingham during the time you were leader of the Circuit. You have a duty to ensure that all people are defended properly when you are leader.

A. One of my duties is to see that the professional conduct of the members of my Circuit is above reproach.

Q. Including competence?

A. Yes, of course, the question of competence is a difficult one as you will well know.

Q. It is now a ground for discipline by the Bar Council.

A. Yes. There was a good deal of debate because, as I understood it... and I think this is a matter which has been reported on by the Royal Commission ... the Royal Commission were very concerned about the competence at the Bar.

Q. Are you concerned?

A. Of course I am.

Q. If you, as leader, became aware that people were being channelled to incompetent barristers in Birmingham would you have done something about it?

A. Yes, if a complaint was made about it. It is a very difficult thing to judge whether a barrister who had passed his exams and had been called to the Bar is competent or incompetent.

Q. You know about plea bargaining in Birmingham, do you not?

A. I know a lot about plea bargaining.

Q. Have you done some yourself, have you engaged in plea bargaining yourself?

A. It depends what you mean.

Q. Let me put it to you. Do you remember the University of Birmingham research some years ago which stated: "Plea bargaining was rife at the hands of the Birmingham Bar where people were being invited to plead guilty in return for a lesser sentence"?

A. I had two long conversations with Doctors McConville and Baldwin who were the authors of that book. When the book was in draft form I had a considerable amount of conversation with them and the matter was discussed at very considerable length.

Q. Do you accept that any member of the Bar has a right to be concerned with the quality of competence afforded to prisoners?

A. I have already answered that "Yes".

Q. Do you therefore agree that any member of the Bar has a right to be concerned not only about competence in court, but concerned about how prisoners are being treated?

A. Of course.

Q. The first letter that I wrote was on the 25th September. Before Mr Jonas ever made contact with you, you received a copy of my letter from me, did you not, in Birmingham?

A. Just a moment. (The Witness looked through his file for the relevant document.) I know you did send copies of this letter because I believe you sent a copy of your letter to the Senate.

Q. That is right.

A. I have not any covering letter in my file indicating I got a copy direct from you.

Q. My letter is dated the 25th September.

A. Yes, I have got the original from Mr. Jonas. He wrote to me.

Q. Do you know that Mr. Jonas is one of the men I accused?

A. I did not know when this letter was written.

Q. No, but you knew before the 4th, before you complained, that Mr Jonas was one of those I was accusing.

THE CHAIRMAN: Mr Narayan, you said something a minute ago which appears to me possibly to be one of importance, perhaps more so than the discussion on plea bargaining and that is that you sent a copy of the letter to the Senate on the 25th September, is that right?

NARAYAN: Yes, that is acknowledged in a letter from Mr Cox to the Senate.

THE CHAIRMAN: It is pointed out to me by Mr. Mota Singh that the copy in my bundle acknowledges receipt by the Senate on the

26th.

MR POWNALL: I do not know whether I can help Mr. Narayan, but the Senate has in its file a copy of the letter dated the 25th September and it was received at the Senate on the 26th. It is not in your bundle.

THE CHAIRMAN: No, but what I have got in my bundle is a photostat with the Senate receipt stamp on it.

NARAYAN: I am most grateful to my learned friend. (To the Witness): We know the Senate got a copy of my letter on the 26th , but did you not also yourself, the very next day, the 26th, receive a copy of my letter from me?

A. I have not any note of that in my file, but it is quite possible that I did. I do not think I would keep more than one copy of the letter, but I do not find any covering letter from you.

Q. Let us put it this way. By the time George Jonas had sent you a copy of my letter, when you saw it from Jonas it was not the first time you had seen it.

A. Yes, it was. I am sure of that because Mr. Jonas spoke to me, first of all, on the telephone.

Q. At home?

A. I cannot remember where it was, I think I was probably in London.

Q. I am putting ...

A. If I could have a moment to think, I will try to remember where I was at the end of September, 1978. (Pause) I think the probability was that I was in London. You will see, from Mr Jonas's letter dated the 28th September, the first paragraph reads: "As suggested by you I have written to you both in London and in Birmingham in the hope that you will receive one letter on Friday morning." I was obviously on the move.

Q. At any rate you now accept that I sent a copy of my letter, as I wrote to the Law Society and as I wrote to the Press, to the Bar Council?

A. As I recall you did because I remember that at some stage at the end of September I think I was told actually in the Senate Offices that a letter had been sent by you to the Senate.

Q. What I want to ask you is this. You did not move to complain at all until the 5th October, is that right?

A. Can you help me about the day of the week?

Q. I can help you by showing you your handwriting. (Document handed to the Witness). Is that your own handwriting?

A. Yes, that is right. You might understand, Mr Narayan, there is no magic in the use of the christian name; it depends upon the relationship of the parties writing. Generally speaking when I communicate with solicitors, unless they are personal friends, I use their surname.

Q. You have never called me "Rudy", have you?

THE CHAIRMAN: I suspect you have not called him "Phillip" either. Let us get on with something that really concerns us.

NARAYAN: I have wanted to call him Phillip for years, but he would not let me. (To the Witness): You now accept that the first time you wrote about my letter was the 5th October.

A. Yes, I wrote a letter dated the 5th October and I have my photographed copy of that letter which was in my own handwriting.

Q. What I am asking you is this. Between the 25th September, when I wrote, and the 5th October, when you wrote – do you follow what I am putting to you?

A. I hear the question, between the 25th and the 5th.

Q. Let me re-phrase it. The first time you ever took any action about this letter was the 5th October.

A. It seems that the first time I put pen to paper was the 5th October.

Q. By then you knew my second letter accusing Jonas, among others, had been sent.

A. Yes, I think it was dated the 4th. I of course had not, when I wrote the letter on the 5th, seen that.

THE CHAIRMAN: Was a copy of this letter also sent to the Senate?

NARAYAN: Yes, and Philip Cox, QC.

THE CHAIRMAN: That was on the 4th October, was it?

NARAYAN: Yes.

THE WITNESS: I think one of the problems, so far as the copies that were sent to me are concerned, Mr Narayan, is that I think you sent them addressed to 3 Fountain Court, instead of to my London Chambers.

NARAYAN: Would you now accept that copies of the letters were sent to you by me the moment I wrote them?

A. I imagine so, yes.

Q. When you wrote on the 5th, the first paragraph of your letter to the Senate begins in this way....

THE CHAIRMAN: You had better supply us with a copy of the letter.

THE WITNESS: This is a three page letter.

NARAYAN: It may be we can take advantage of the luncheon

adjournment to do that.

THE CHAIRMAN: If you can agree and put together a bundle of anything anybody wants to refer to it will be much easier to follow.

NARAYAN (To the Witness): Mr. Cox, would you have before you Bundle B which has just been exhibited? (Same handed to the Witness). It is a bundle of letters from prisoners. Will you find one from Mr. Ginda?

A. One moment, Mr. Narayan.

THE CHAIRMAN: What page is this?

NARAYAN: Page 2.

THE WITNESS: I have that.

Q. Do you see that that letter, from a prisoner in Birmingham prison, is addressed to me?

A. Yes, should I read it?

Q. I will read it and you follow it. "As you will no doubt be aware from my present address I am in trouble with the authorities. I am and have been awaiting trial since the 8th November, 1977. I am charged with the murder of my wife Vedya Devi Ginda, who disappeared on the 29th October, 1973.

"I am absolutely innocent of these charges against me. Therefore, I want you to act on behalf of me as soon as possible. At present my solicitors are A. Mervyn Williams, Pipers Meadow, Bilston, West Midlands. Tel. (0902) 42613, they have been doing their best to help me since last year, but I am not very happy with the way they have handled my case.

"I will be seeking your help in due course and hope I will hear from you at your earliest convenience.

"First I did not know that you have moved from London to Birmingham."

A. That letter is not dated, I was just wondering whether....

Q. The second letter is 5/3. "I am sorry I have not replied to your letter of the 4th October 1978 earlier than now as my date of trial is getting very near after 13 months long waiting in remand...

THE CHAIRMAN: What pages are you on?

MR SINGH: Who is it from?

NARAYAN: It is from Ginda.

THE WITNESS: There is only one letter from Ginda in this bundle.

MR. SINGH: It is not in this bundle, we do not have it.

NARAYAN: I will read it and furnish you with copies in due course. "It was a good excuse for my solicitors to talk me out of my willingness for you to act for me in my defence. I tried my best to make my solicitors listen to me but it was no use being too soft-hearted and not knowing enough about the law fields as my rights.

Now I cannot help myself thinking about the mistakes I have made. The results and the ways that things had gone in the court has left depressing remark on me and my family. We all have been left deprived of our rights by the police and my solicitors. There is nothing I can do about it in the prison as my children are too young to help me and I have no one outside helpful to me. Although my solicitors told me it was travesty of justice and have appealed against my conviction but I am not happy about the things was going against me and I do not understand why my solicitor let me acting on my defence on my request for you. Although I am not good at defending myself I feel there are more than enough grounds for my re-trial and feel if there happen to be re-trial then I want you to act for me in my defence." (To the Witness): Can I ask you this. If you knew that prisoners, regardless of race, were being deprived in this way of counsel of their choice, would you have mounted a campaign against the Law Society?

A. I should want to know a little more about it, I am afraid Mr. Narayan, because it is not clear to me. Had Mr. Ginda written to the Law Society or had he made any complaint about the conduct of his solicitors apart from the complaint to you?

Q. I am asking you questions and you are to answer them. If you knew that prisoners, regardless of race or colour, were being deprived of their human rights in this way, would you, as leader of the Circuit, have mounted a campaign against the Law Society?

A. If I had known this was happening I should have reported the matter to the President of the Law Society or if a complaint had been made to me I should have...

Q. Referred it to the President of the Law Society?

A. Yes.

Q. Obviously, when you reported it your language would have been fairly refined?

A. I should have reported the matter.

Q. Yes, in a proper way. But if you had been complaining about this over the years, as the years went by do you think your language may have got a little bit stronger with every passing year?

A. It is difficult to say.

NARAYAN: Supposing, Mr. Cox, you were complaining over the years and the Law Society did not do a single thing, would you not go to the press and expose this state of affairs?

A. If I had been complaining to the President of the Law Society about what I thought to be professional misconduct and nothing was done about it, I think possibly I might have taken other steps before going to the press but there might come a time when the matter ought to be ventilated publicly.

Q. You agree with me that this is a matter of public interest?

A Of course it is.

Q. You know that you wrote me a letter saying the Bar cannot investigate solicitors.

A. Yes.

Q. Do you know that the Chairman of the Bar Council caused such a letter to be written to me saying he cannot investigate solicitors?

A. No.

Q. I will invite your attention to it.

THE WITNESS: I do not recall seeing such a letter.

NARAYAN: Mr. Cox, the Chairman of the Bar is based in London, so London refuses and Birmingham refuses. Do you know I have also got a letter from the London Law Society saying that they cannot investigate it?

A. No, I do not.

Q. Do you accept this, that there is no machinery at the Bar for investigating the conduct of solicitors?

A. I think that is right.

Q. So if we want solicitors to be investigated the Bar cannot help?

A. All the Bar can do is to draw the attention of the Law Society to the alleged misconduct of the solicitor as I understand it.

Q. In this case did you draw the attention of the Law Society to my complaints?

A. I have not received any complaint from you ever.

Q. When you heard that the letter of mine was sent before the Senate, after Mr. George Jonas sent you a copy, did it appear to you that I appeared to be complaining?

A. Certainly.

Q. What have you done about it?

A. You had yourself sent a copy of that letter to the Senate and I drew the attention of the Senate to it immediately.

A. As leader of the Circuit, are you not under a duty to assist a member of the Bar to complain?

A. Speaking generally, yes, but you see a member of the Bar, if he or anyone wishes to make a complaint about another member of the Bar or a solicitor, he has his right of access to the professional body, whether it be the Senate or the Law Society. I was leader of the Circuit for four years and there were a number of complaints to the Senate or, I imagine, to the Law Society from members of my Circuit during that period but they were not channelled through me; they would go straight to the professional body.

Q. Do you accept that if there is a complaint of racial discrimination affecting members of the Bar you have a public and professional duty to espouse that complaint to its logical conclusion?

A. It depends upon the circumstances. If the complaint is sent to me simply as a copy of a complaint made to the Senate I would not regard it as my duty to espouse the complaint.

Q. Do you want there to be racial discrimination?

A. No, if there is any racial discrimination I regret it and anything I could do to put an end to it I should do.

Q. Do you accept, as of today, that no one at the Bar of England and Wales has done anything about my complaints?

A. I know this, Mr. Narayan, that when you wrote to me and you wrote to the Chairman of the Bar in the earlier part of 1978 saying that you wished to open Chambers in Birmingham, I invited you to become a member of the circuit. You write to me a letter in the earlier part of that year....

Q. Saying I would come and join your circuit....

A. Just one moment, you wrote to me on the 12th May. I do not know whether this letter is before the Tribunal.

Q. I see you have got a cutting of me from the Birmingham Mail and a photograph of me.

A. Yes.

Q. Do you keep a file on me, Mr. Cox?

A. I keep a file of the letters that I receive.

Q. And press cuttings?

A. The press cutting is dated May 16th. I think it is my duty, as leader of the circuit, to keep a file in relation to any matter that I consider refers to professional conduct.

Q. Were you considering taking action against me because of that press cutting?

A. No, certainly not. But I was interested to read that press cutting, dated May 16th, in view of the content of your letter dated May 12th.

Q. Before we come to that, would you answer my question? Are you aware of anything that the Bar of England has done to investigate my complaint?

A. I know that so far as the Senate is concerned, the Senate had the details of your complaint which you made to the press and to the Law Society. The Law Society is the appropriate body to investigate this complaint.

Q. Look at this letter from the Law Society, Mr. Cox?

THE CHAIRMAN: Mr. Narayan, you must be conscious that the charge against you is now limited to a very narrow matter indeed. I am allowing you as much latitude as possible, but really these matters have got nothing whatever to do with the main charge. The simple question is (1) was it an offensive letter and (2) if it was, does it amount to conduct unbecoming?

NARAYAN: Is there not a second charge, sending a copy to the press?

THE CHAIRMAN: Yes, sending a copy to the press. If it was not offensive – or it was not unbecoming, then as I understand the framing of the charges, the second charge goes too. That is right, Mr. Pownall, is it not?

MR POWNALL: That is right, certainly.

NARAYAN: Mr. Cox, let me ask you this. You, when you were leader of the Circuit, would have been in a very powerful position compared to me.

A. Yes, of course, but you were not a member of my Circuit and that was one of the difficulties I felt, because it is not easy for me, as leader of one Circuit, to have dealings with you, who were a member of the South Eastern Circuit, at the time.

THE CHAIRMAN: I am going to ask a question. You wrote to the Law Society with a complaint, is that right?

NARAYAN: Yes.

THE CHAIRMAN: You got a reply from the London Law Society saying that they could not investigate it?

NARAYAN: No, I wrote separately and later to London sending them more letters than I had informed Birmingham about. Having failed in Birmingham I tried my luck with London.

THE CHAIRMAN: London said they could not help?

NARAYAN: That is right.

THE CHAIRMAN: So, at that stage, you had got a lack of interest, at the very least, from both London and Birmingham Law Societies, is that right?

NARAYAN: What I got was confirmation that there was no machinery for them to move at my instance.

THE CHAIRMAN: Birmingham, presumably, had not said there was no machinery.

NARAYAN: No, what Birmingham had said was this. After four days Mr. Jonas had recommended that they be sent on to London excluding the complaint against him, Jonas. Within four days the Birmingham Law Society wrote back to me saying there was no point investigating these matters. It is in one sentence: "I have now had the opportunity of investigating the matters of which you complain and I have no justification for taking the matters any further."

THE CHAIRMAN: Have you, since you were turned down by the Law Society in London and the Law Society in Birmingham, requested Mr. Cox to take up the cudgels on your behalf?

NARAYAN: No, because Mr. Cox....

THE CHAIRMAN: I only want an answer to the question. Have you asked the Senate to take up the cudgels on your behalf?

THE RESPONDENT: Since being refused, no.

THE CHAIRMAN: With the Law Society?

NARAYAN: Not since they have all refused because I did not think there was any point in asking them all over again. (To the Witness): Do you know something called The Commission for Racial Equality?

A. Yes.

Q. Are you aware I have made complaints to them too about this same matter? Are you aware that I have asked for a full, formal public inquiry into racialism in the legal profession?

A. No, indeed I had never, until I was communicated with by the Birmingham Law Society, any knowledge at all of the allegation of racialism apart from the suggestion that Mr. Charles Noel made, many years ago, that he was being discriminated against by the Birmingham Prosecuting Solicitor.

Q. Do you accept that England is inherently racialist?

A. No, I do not accept that.

Q. Let us phrase it another way. Knowing my experience in the criminal court as well as you do.....

A. Let me make it clear, I know you have considerable ability in the criminal courts.

Q. That is very kind. Knowing of that reputation, can you see that these refusals can be justification on the grounds of incompetence by me?

A. When you say "these" you are holding up a bundle of letters.

Q. A single refusal, if you like, Ginda, the murder case we just read, can you see that any one solicitor can justify refusing to send me a case of this criminal type on the grounds of my incompetence?

A. No. If a solicitor refused to brief you on the gounds of your incompetence, my view would be that that would not be justified.

Q. If a solicitor refused a client counsel of his choice unprofessionally, as we both agree, and if you want to see a multi-racial Bar, what justification do you think this solicitor can have in the whole of England for refusing to send me a case at the specific request of the client?

A. I tried to answer that question this morning. It depends on the case.

THE WITNESS: If it was a criminal case in the ordinary field I think I have already answered the question. Other things being equal, the solicitor would not have any grounds for refusing to brief you at the express request of a client.

NARAYAN: First of all, he would be in breach of his professional duty if he did so refuse?

A. Certainly.

Q. Secondly, he of course would not be dealing with a beginner of a barrister?

A. You are not a beginner, you are 10 or 12 years' call or more than that.

Q. Yes. This case of Ginda, the murder case, did it go to someone in your chambers eventually?

A. I am afraid I do not know. I have never heard of the case until I saw the correspondence in this matter. I know nothing about him myself.

Q. Let me come to how you came to make complaint against me. First of all, we established before lunch that you did not move to complain until the 5th October.

A. I certainly wrote a letter on the 5th October to the Secretary of the Senate, but I may have spoken on the telephone to the Senate before that, I simply do not remember. I may have, indeed I believe I did, visit the Senate before that.

Q. According to this file of papers you have here, the first time you complained in writing, certainly, was the 5th October or sought to complain?

A. Yes. You see, I do not keep a copy of every letter I write. One of the problems that I faced as leader of the Circuit....

THE CHAIRMAN: Will the public kindly keep quiet, there are too many people in this room for the slightest noise to be made.

A. ...is I do not have a secretarial back-up and I have to do the job myself. If I keep a copy I have to have a piece of carbon at hand and write it in longhand.

NARAYAN: Let us put it this way. From the evidence you have in your own file today, the first time you moved to complain against me in writing was the 5th October, yes or no?

A. I am not sure about that because I do recall writing a letter to the Secretary of the Senate, a copy of which I did not keep.

Q. Perhaps the Senate would produce that letter if it is in existence.

A I think you showed me a copy of the letter which I wrote this morning.

THE CHAIRMAN: You may take it, Mr. Narayan, that I have no evidence of any complaint before the 5th October and I act on the evidence.

NARAYAN: Yes. The next thing, Mr Cox, is this. You know by now that my letter had been lying at the Bar Council, where I had sent it, from the 26th September.

A. Yes if you say so, I did not know that.

Q. When you rang up the Bar Council to complain about me they told you: "We have already got Narayan's letter here".

A. Yes. Whether it was on the telephone or whether I called in, I do not know.

Q. You know that my letter was at the Senate between the 26th September and the 5th October when you wrote?

Q. What I am asking you is this. Here you are, my letter is in the Senate and nobody in the Senate found it offensive, do you follow? At least we have not got anybody coming here today from the Senate.

A. I cannot speak for the Senate. You see, Mr. Jonas had asked me to take action.

Q. We will come to Mr. Jonas. That is George, is it not? There is my letter lying at the Senate and nobody at the Senate has complained to the Professional Conduct Committee about me because otherwise we would have had it here. You know that both my letters were written to the President, do you not?

A. The President of the Birmingham Law Society. I have copies of two letters, the first letter of the 25th was addressed to the President of the Birmingham Law Society and the second letter was addressed simply "Dear President".

Q. You knew Mr. George Jonas was not the President at the time.

A. Yes, I cannot recall who was.

Q. You knew Mr. George Jonas was not the President.

Q. He was the Vice President, wasn't he?

A. He cannot have been.

Q. Therefore my complaints were not addressed to Jonas, they were addressed to the President, and you knew my second letter accused Jonas.

A. It says so.

Q. You knew that when I wrote to the President he was alive and well and living in Birmingham.

A. I did not know where he was, all I knew was that he was on holiday.

Q. When you got the first letter "Dear Phillip" signed "George" of the 28th September, you will see in the fourth paragraph he refers to speaking to Mr. Taylor who told him that a copy of my letter to the President had been sent to the Birmingham Post.

A. The short fourth paragraph, yes.

Q. The third paragraph: "As it happened we had an officers' meeting... and it was decided that the President would write to Mr. Narayan..." Do you see that?

A. Yes.

A. Yes, I think I must make it clear that although I had known Mr. Jonas for many years he was not a personal friend, indeed I have never attended any sort of social gathering outside the profession of any sort.

Q. How does he come to address you as "Phillip"?

A. That is a matter for him.

Q. You did not object to that?

A. No, I would not; it would be common courtesy not to object.

Q. It would be proper, would it not, for an official letter from the Law Society to go to your Chambers addressed as "Mr. Cox, Leader of the Circuit"?

A. No, if you look at the letter of the 28th, the reason why it was addressed to me at my home address was to make sure I got it quickly because there is a danger, as you know, that if it is sent to 3, Fountain Court in Birmingham some days can easily pass before it gets into my possession.

Q. Why did he write to your home address a second time?

A. It may be I suggested that he should, I do not know.

Q. Here we are and before you write you now realise I am complaining about Mr. George Jonas.

A. When I saw the second letter, yes.

Q. Do you take the view that if a barrister complains against a solicitor or if anyone complains about anyone else, the complaint should be allowed to run its natural course?

A. It must be investigated.

Q. What must not happen is that a person who is accused in a complaint has a chance, as it were, of deflecting the course of natural justice.

A. Let us look at this first letter to you.

MR. SINGH: Mr. Narayan, are we going to hear about preventing a preliminary investigation by the Law Society?

NARAYAN: If you look at the totality of the evidence, the phone calls, the private letters to Mr. Cox's home, Mr. Jonas speaking to the press and Mr. Jonas telling the President to stifle his complaints and proceed on the others to London, that is a stifling of an enquiry in my submission.

MR SINGH: I think you have made the point.

NARAYAN (To the Witness): What I ask you is this. Did you realise, at the time, that you were being used to stifle an inquiry into unprofessional conduct by Mr. George Jonas?

A. I did not consider that I was being used in any way and I would not be party to being used.

Q. Do you now see that perhaps unwittingly you have allowed yourself to be used to stifle an inquiry into unprofessional conduct by

Mr George Jonas, among others?

A. I do not think I was used in that way, but if you can satisfy me, if it is relevant, I will certainly listen to any question you wish to put.

Q. Look at the second letter of the 6th October.

THE CHAIRMAN: What page?

NARAYAN: Page 111 in Bundle K. (To the Witness): Looking at that letter, do you see the first paragraph refers to him enclosing to you a further letter from me?

A. Yes.

Q. That further letter from me, you now accept, shows me complaining against Jonas.

A. Yes.

Q. Do you see in that first paragraph he is denying the allegation against his firm?

A. Yes, I have read this letter.

Q. Do you see, having given his reasons and explanation, in paragraph 4 he says this: "So far as the other complaints are concerned..."

A. This is the fifth paragraph.

Q. Yes. "So far as the other complaints are concerned I am suggesting to the President that they ought to be referred to the Professional Purposes Committee of the Law Society in London."

A. Yes.

Q. When you read that did it appear to you that Jonas had strangled a complaint against him at birth, but sent on the others concerning other people?

A. It did not occur to me then and, reading the letter even now, I cannot see that.

NARAYAN: (To the Witness): Do you see this. I, having complained and named Mr. Jonas in my letter, the accused man is now writing to you? Do you follow?

A. He is simply denying the charge you made against him.

Q. Since I had complained about him to the President, do you think it right and proper for the President to be writing to you, if at all?

A. I find it very difficult to answer that.

NARAYAN (To the Witness): When Mr. Jonas wrote to you denying the very accusation I was making against him, did it occur to you to say "Look here, George, I am not going to have any further correspondence with you; this complaint must take its natural course"?

A. No, I did what I thought was right.

Q. Why did you not say to this man: "Look here, a member of the

Bar has complained about you. I am not going to be party to receiving private letters from you, things must take their natural course"?

A. No, I do not think that is right....

NARAYAN: The other thing is this. Bearing in mind the President was the man to whom I addressed both letters, though we have letters from Mr. Jonas saying, for example, in his second letter to you "Dear Phillip . . . Yours, George . . . This must be stopped", the President has never written to you complaining about my letter, has he?

A. No, I understood Mr. Jonas was writing to me on the advice of the President.

Q. That was what Mr. Jonas told you. If it was official, why was he writing "Phillip" and "George" to your home address?

A. Mr Narayan...

NARAYAN: Can I put this to you about my first letter. If the President had complained to you one can see the logic because I had written to the President, do you follow?

A. Yes.

Q. When I write to the President and the accused man, Jonas, complains to you, why do you complain because the President has not?

A. I had been asked to.

Q. Because you had been asked to by the man you knew since 1950, George Jonas.

A. That had nothing to do with it, it did not have the slightest to do with it, the fact that I had known Mr. Jonas since 1950.

Q. You accept that the President, the man to whom that letter was addressed, has never complained about my writing.

A. Complained to whom?

Q. The President has never complained to anyone about my letters.

A. The President of the Birmingham Law Society?

Q. Of course.

A. As I indicated earlier, I understood that I was receiving these letters, which were on the letter heading of the Birmingham Law Society, on behalf of the Birmingham Law Society and I conceived it my duty to pass on these complaints to the Professional Conduct Committee.

Q. Do you take the view that the Vice-President may write officially on behalf of the Law Society denying allegations made against him?

A. Would you re-phrase that?

Q. Do you take the vie that the vice-President, just because he uses the headed papers of the Law Society, can write to you officially and deny allegations against himself?

A. It is a matter for him how he writes. If he had not denied the allegations his silence might have been construed as consent.

Q. Let me ask you another question. You have never enquired of the President of the Birmingham Law Society, have you, whether he found this letter offensive? You have never made that enquiry, have you?

A. It did not seem to me to be a matter for me to enquire of him; it is a matter for the professional body.

Q. Can we take it your answer is that you have never enquired?

A. No, I have never enquired.

All the four charges founded on Cox's "complaint" were thrown out without calling on Rudy to reply! This cross-examination, conducted historically before the world's Press, Radio and Television, is now a matter of public record. (See "Barrister on Trial" [1980], Hansib Publishing.)

(2) The Advocacy of Challenge – Bar Council Trial, April, 1980.

I wish to make it clear that we do not repeat this speech from "Barrister on Trial" (Hansib Publishing, April 1980) to revive old quarrels or to seek to reassert the truth of matters stated publicly four years ago but only because we view this speech as highly instructive of the kind of advocacy we would wish others to aspire to.

This is very much a subjective speech, but a minor classic in its own right and highly educational on how to use the English language in machine-gun style!

Arif Ali

Now, like the community in Bristol last week, a man can take only so much. Just because one is a barrister does not mean one has no feelings or that one is not flesh and blood. Despite your contempt and denigration I am human too. And when I wrote that first letter I wrote not just as a human being angry with solicitors who would deprive me of the right to earn my livelihood according to merit and ability; I wrote also because the cause of the prisoner has always been a total commitment with me. To think of my brothers languishing there in prison and their wishes being treated with arrogance and contempt is too much for one man to be called upon to bear after ten years. But I wrote also as a barrister who states here and now that it is in the highest tradition of the lawyer through history to take the most vigorous and public stand against injustices against the common man. And if you are unable to find that such vigorous action is in the highest traditions of the English Bar then the English Bar offends against the highest standards and traditions of universal law.

You query the words "experience and distinction". My answer is, these words are true and secondly they are necessary to prove prejudice, especially to the public. Solicitors' refusals to send briefs to barristers without experience and distinction can be rationalised but what answer do they have for refusing to instruct me?

Apart from which, I knew that back in 1973, Phillip Cox QC had presided over a meeting of the Midland Circuit when refusal to instruct barrister Charles Noel was justified on the grounds of alleged incompetence. So, knowing of this case I *knew* that the only way to get public support was by stating that such rationalisation could not possibly apply to me. If you think I did it to advertise myself, I, of all barristers in this whole land, do not need to advertise. My competence and commitment is already well-known.

The final words about this first letter. I was complaining about discrimination. Since the first Race Relations Act, it is illegal and those who offend should be prosecuted. I am entitled to complain. Because it is a matter of Statute it is a matter of public concern. If the public is being denied a fundamental right by the legal profession it is in the highest traditions of the Bar to tell them so. A barrister who knows that the profession is behaving against the public interest and keeps quiet about it should not be a barrister. By this standard, all the barristers in Birmingham should be disbarred. I have served the public interest by revealing and exposing an unsatisfactory state of affairs. In doing so, not only have I not broken any laws, I have officially urged through complaint the pursuit of illegality through the laws of the land.

What I have stated is the truth. If it is offensive, so be it but it cannot be conduct unbecoming of a barrister.

Either I have broken the law or I have not. Either I have spoken the truth or I have not. Desperate situations call for vigorous words. Shakespeare and GBS knew this. If I am being attacked with a murderous weapon the law says that homicide in self-defence is justifiable homicide. Here I was being strangled professionally on all sides and the prisoners too. This is like a man being strangled and he starts cussing his attacker. He has not broken any law but the Bar Council gets him for cussing since cussing is conduct unbecoming to a barrister!

The final word about this letter is this. When I declared war against the Birmingham Law Society, I thought in my innocence that the Bar Council would join in on my side because I thought that the Bar would never stand by and let one of their own be treated this way. I forgot for the moment the history of discrimination of the Bar itself and forgot also the politics of Kith and Kin. I forgot as well that the Bar in Birmingham has a vested interest in joining in on the Law Society's side since it is the Birmingham Bar that reaps the fruits of such discrimination.

These Club Rules have got to go. They are obsolete and irrelevant. They have no place in the case of a profession that flourishes at the expense of the prisoner. A barrister is entitled to protest. He is also entitled to defend himself. Freedom of speech and the right to protest is the right of every citizen, regardless of occupation or status.

Freedom of speech and human rights take precedence over club rules and where they conflict with the liberty of the subject and the rights of the citizen, such rules are clearly obnoxious and repugnant to a democratic society and cannot prevail against the fundamental rights of the barrister as citizen.

My Final Preliminary Remarks Are These:

The community has begun to fight back against oppression and discrimination. You take our people, you exploit, suppress, harass and hound them and deny them their rights and then when they have nowhere else to turn, when their backs are up against the wall we start cussing! And when we start cussing after years of frustration and embitterment you step forward to me and say: "Bad form old boy, you must not be rude to solicitors. After all we at the Bar have prostituted and prostrated ourselves for years before solicitors so that we will get the work. One thing you will not be allowed to do is to be rude to the very solicitor who takes your work away from you and gives it to us and one thing you will not be allowed to do is to stop those same solicitors from denying the rights of black prisoners. After all solicitors are our keepers and paymasters. If you write a letter to me, Phillip Cox QC, Leader of the Midland Circuit, I will do nothing. But the moment George Jonas urges me, by Jove, watch me nail that bounder Narayan to the cross. I, Phillip Cox QC will not say, as one member of my Chambers did say that "All Asian Barristers are Rogues" but I will act, not against complaints of racial discrimination lodged by a barrister but I will act on complaints of rudeness lodged by my solicitor George Jonas."

Now let us examine the totality of the conduct that taints this entire trial and I will now demonstrate how everyone involved in these matters has acted with something less than the integrity and fairmindedness that the public is entitled to demand of the legal professions.

In these matters, it is a matter of total regret to me that three very eminent Jewish lawyers have played major roles. It is a matter of deep personal regret to me because the Jews should know better from their own history of racialist persecution and harassment. But I regret that solicitor George Jonas who laid the complaint, Barrister Peter Taylor QC who chaired the PCC which laid the charges and Bar Council

Chairman David Hirst QC who refused to investigate my complaints have found it possible despite their own race's suffering from persecution, to conduct themselves in this way. It is also a matter of total regret to me because, in my view, the majority of Jewish people in high positions have a tremendous depth of understanding and sympathy for the sufferings of our people and it is my hope that the Jewish community will convey to these three august gentlemen their own views of their conduct in these matters.

In 1978, when I first set up our annex in Birmingham, I was unaware of this little bit of Mr. Jonas's personal history so that when he personally assured me in writing and in person that Jasper Antonie Morrison, a defendant, had wrongfully accused his firm of such discrimination against me, I, knowing that Mr. Jonas was supposed to be a well-known solicitor in Birmingham, was happy to accept in due course his personal assurance that his firm had not discriminated against me.

In any event, when I wrote that letter of 25th September 1978, it was within my knowledge that Mr. George Jonas's firm was then being accused by a prisoner of discriminating against me in favour of a barrister in Birmingham.

My letter was addressed to the President of the Law Society, Mr. R.J. Garratt. It was not addressed to nor was it intended for Mr. George Jonas who would have known by then that his firm had been accused of discrimination because when the prisoner made that complaint, Mr. Jonas's assistant Mr. Ewan Smith was present, that same Mr. Smith who appeared with Mr. Jonas before the Race Relations Board in 1973.

I waited for a reply. But I made sure that I had sent copies of the letter to the Bar Council, to the local Circuit Leader, one Phillip Cox QC, and also to the Press.

The Bar Council received my letter and did nothing about my complaints. To this very day they have refused to act. It is a matter of deep regret to me that the Chairman of the Bar Council, who I believe was then Mr. David Hirst QC, refused to investigate my complaints. The Bar is supposed to be the barristers' trade union in that they will lobby for more money for barristers but when some barristers are being denied the right to earn that money, they say they can do nothing. Such blatant hypocrisy about minority rights within the legal profession has to stop.

I also sent a copy of my letter to Phillip Cox QC. To this day he has done nothing about my complaints.

By 28th September, 1978, three days later, nobody at the Bar Council in London had found the letter to be "offensive" or in breach of any of the professional rules of etiquette. This I submit is a most important point since I had sent my letter to the senior barrister in all England, the Chairman of the Bar Council, and he had found nothing worthy of complaint in that letter.

It is also of importance that Phillip Cox QC himself found nothing to complain about in that letter otherwise I presume he himself would have moved to complain without needing any persuasion from George Jonas.

So, I submit, those responsible at the Bar themselves found nothing offensive in the letter and nobody moved to complain.

However, the accused solicitor Jonas, whose clerk Mr. Smith had told him by now of the prisoner's allegations, telephoned Phillip Cox QC on 27th September, 1978, and discussed the matter with Cox QC.

Phillip Cox QC then advised George Jonas to write to Cox. Remember, my letter had been addressed to the President not to Mr. Jonas. The President himself has never once complained to anyone that he found this letter to be offensive. Yet I am charged with sending an offensive letter to the President. If the President had indeed found that letter offensive, why had he not complained? The only man who had complained is the 1973 Race Relations Board defendant, Mr. George Jonas.

Now let us analyse Mr. Jonas's private letter to Phillip Cox QC.

The first question about that letter is this: Does it establish that the President of the Law Society found it to be offensive? Does it establish Mr. George Jonas himself found it offensive? I ask again, as Jesus Christ did, 1980 years ago this Easter, when he asked it of Pilate before they nailed him to the cross, (it seems that Easter time is a very popular time for crucifixions) I ask as Christ did: "When did truth ever become offensive, except to the guilty ear?"

As long as I keep my protest within the laws of the land, as long as I am exposing an unjust state of affairs, it is in the highest traditions of the legal profession to speak out loudly, fearlessly and publicly.

This letter of Jonas, was it an official complaint or a personal letter? If the President found it offensive why has he not officially complained? How does it come about that the Vice President is complaining in this manner?

Why does Jonas have to speak to the Press in "diplomatic terms?" These complaints are serious matters. Why did the President not speak to the Press? What is the accused man Jonas doing talking to the Press in diplomatic terms and writing and telephoning one of Her Majesty's Queen's Counsel in this way?

This man's first three actions speak for themselves.

And you bring me here to face these nonsensical charges without having the decency to bring this man Jonas face-to-face with me? Is he to be allowed to stay in Birmingham while one of Her Majesty's Queen's Counsel is being dragged here to do his work for him? If Mr. Jonas is a man with an honest complaint, bring him here before me today so his motivations in prompting Cox QC can be laid before the Press and the community leadership assembled here.

This man Jonas occupies today the Presidency of the Birmingham Law Society and people are being invited to trust him.

He occupies a position of respect and trust in Birmingham society and people in Birmingham are being encouraged to respect people like the local Presidents of Law Societies. If Mr. Jonas finds the conduct of a member of the Bar to be worthy of complaint then why does he not show his face and stand up in the public gaze and state what his complaint is?

The position that the Bar is in today is that Phillip Cox QC is acting as complainant for a solicitor. Since when does Her Majesty's Queen's Counsel complain for solicitors? Why does the leader of the Midlands Circuit, who himself does not at first complain about the letter, suddenly move into action at the prompting of Mr. George Jonas?

Now on 28th September 1978, the President of the Law Society writes to me.

He states that he "has no knowledge" and seeks information from me. He speaks that he has "caused" a copy of the letter to be sent to Cox QC.

Time Out magazine indicates that my allegations are true. These solicitors are in breach of their own rules. Why has the Law Society not prosecuted a few?

Now that we know that these solicitors have been acting against their own professional rules and against the Universal Declaration of Human Rights and even against Magna Carta, have they also been acting against the Race Relations Act? But the Bar cannot sit here and put the blame on the Law Society. Until the past twelve months the Bar itself has deliberately and wickedly and unlawfully kept blacks and working class people and women too, out of the legal profession and has aided and abetted the Law Society to discriminate against prisoners. It has been a very profitable and unholy alliance between the Bar and the Law Society. Therefore, while the Bar is just beginning to put its own house in order on this question its own hands are stained with the blood of the barristers who were systematically refused places by the barristers' Heads of Chambers (except the late Sir Dingle Foot QC). In the past twelve to eighteen months, ever since September 1978, the Bar has been very frantically seeking tame house-blacks for an emergency window-dressing operation.

So now tell me, have solicitors behaved in this way against white barristers? Then why, despite my proven excellence and noted personal beauty, why except for race and colour, do they do this to me? Don't tell me it's because I am not competent. Otherwise I shall be again forced to write even more letters to the Press launching my complaint from the platform of a barrister of experience and distinction.

Now on 4th October I wrote again to the President of the Law Society. He had asked for details so I gave him details. Such details included the firm of the celebrated Mr. George Jonas, then the Vice-President of the Birmingham Law Society.

This information the Press would have published weeks earlier anyway.

So you can now see the hand of Mr. George Jonas whose finger is on every trigger behind the scenes. He is dealing with this at three levels. With his President, with the Press and with his Phillip Cox QC.

Meanwhile back at the Phillip Cox ranch, it is now 5th October and Cox is in London. Now some eleven days have passed and neither the Bar Council nor Phillip Cox personally have seen anything wrong enough to justify complaint about his first letter.

But my second letter, delivered by hand on 4th October 1978, has really set the cat among the pigeons.

Now again on the 4th October I am writing not to the celebrated George Jonas but the President, a Mr. Garratt, and in that letter it is now plain for all to see, including the President and George Jonas that Jonas is named expressly as one of the accused solicitors.

Now what should the Law Society President do?

He should make sure that no accused solicitor ever gets sight of these letters except perhaps as part of an official enquiry.

It is then and only then, after I have actually named Mr. George Jonas that that leading light of the Birmingham Bar, Mr. Phillip Cox QC, writes a letter to "Arthur".

On 5th October 1978, Cox is stating almost expressly that he does not believe that I have provided any of the particulars requested by the President. But I did, the day before, 4th October. The newspaper article had appeared on 3rd October.

In his letter of 5th October, Cox stated that he is dealing with the Vice-President, the accused solicitor Jonas. Why not deal with the President?

And Cox, writing from London, states that he is told that an extract has appeared in the Birmingham Press. Who told Phillip that this had happened? Did George Jonas ring up Phillip on 4th October? It couldn't have been the President because the President would have told Cox that I had supplied particulars and that I had named Jonas.

Cox in his letter reveals his own personal vexation with me for not joining the Circuit. He further states in this letter that "the time has come when firm action should be taken." So now dear old Phillip Cox is taking up the battle on behalf of George Jonas who proceeds to disappear off the scene after writing one more letter.

George Jonas writes again on 6th October, 1978, after my second letter has been received. Incidentally, such is the relationship between these two that Jonas writes both times to Cox's home address: George Road, Edgbaston. Again, ask yourselves this question. (Never mind the fact that Jonas is writing to "Phillip" at his home address, perhaps Jonas is just very fond of Cox's home address) but the point is this: my second letter, as was the first, was addressed to the President. The President received it and it accuses Jonas, among others. Instead of the President writing to the Leader of the Midland Circuit in both their official capacities as local leader of the Bar and Law Society respectively it is again the accused solicitor George Jonas who is writing to "Phillip."

In this letter George Jonas proceeds to answer the allegation against his firm. He stated that I accepted that the black prisoner's allegation was untrue – this is not the case.

It was only some days later, after Jonas had written to me a letter giving me a personal assurance that it was not true that he met me in Birmingham Crown Court and literally begged me to confirm in writing that I accepted his assurance could not be true. I would not accept any denials or assurances from him now that I saw how he had figured in the prompting of the Bar to silence me from exposing certain things in public. I say he has prompted the local Bar into trying to silence me because he goes on to say that: "This must be stopped." A local solicitor writing a personal letter to one of the Leaders of the Bar of England and Wales to his private home address in these terms?

Further, Jonas in the letter states that so far as "the other complaints" are concerned he has recommended that they should be referred to London. But what has happened to my complaint against him? Does Jonas have the power as well to persuade his President not to proceed with a complaint against him? Is a complaint against Mr. George Jonas simply to be dealt with by Mr. Jonas himself?

And note the P.S. Once again the hand and voice of Mr. George Jonas has reached out.

I trust by now that I have shown that this complaint would never have been made were it not for Mr. George Jonas, a solicitor complained about by others to the Race Relations Board in 1973, and one of the accused solicitors who disenfranchised the Birmingham Law Society of investigating him and got the local Leader of the Bar to do his complaining for him.

So why is he not here today and how can Cox speak for the Law Society?

Now it is the 6th October that Cox shows his hand. Jonas has set the wheels in motion and now Cox takes over.

Cox tells the Secretary of the Senate that he has spoken to George Jonas on the telephone and that both Jonas and Faber say there is no truth in my allegations. I have accused two solicitors, one of them privately telephones Cox. Cox does not enquire of me but accepts the assurance of solicitors, outsiders to the profession. Or are they outsiders really? What kind of Leader is this? His duty is to act fairly and honestly but when I accuse solicitors he disregards my complaints and accepts private assurances from the accused!

Further Cox goes so far as to suggest that Jonas and Faber are willing to give evidence against me (presumably if I am charged). Does this mean that Cox is now, having made complaint, pressuring the Senate to go ahead and charge in the sure knowledge the local solicitors can be counted on to give evidence against me?

What kind of Leader of the Bar is this? To consult with solicitors and to reassure the Senate that they would not be lacking in evidence from the very men I accused?

But note the final sentence. Cox is willing to send his Deputy Leader to a secret meeting of the PCC.

Now what the hell are Cox and the PCC up to?

Why should Cox, Jonas's agent in this complaint, attend a meeting of the PCC when the PCC had to decide whether or not to bring charges that Cox would like to see brought?

Why was I not notified of this meeting and why was I not invited to urge the opposite?

I wrote to Cox on 9th to upbraid him for his total lack of professional conscience.

Now, after all these dealings by frightened men, men who feared me because I was bent on exposing their activities to the public but men who feared me because, as *Time Out* magazine reported, I was popular in the prisons and the clients destined for white Chambers were asking to be defended by me. A lot of money is passing round the Birmingham Bar in the dealing with black people's cases and I was the catalyst of disruption in the sense that I have always encouraged people to demand their rights. Apart from which, there is no single barrister in Birmingham who approaches one tenth of my commitment to defendants and people know this.

And now, the President of the Birmingham Law Society writes to me stating that he had investigated these matters. How extraordinary. Within that very short time and without interviewing a single prisoner and without asking for the letters that I had, he claimed to have completed an investigation! *Time Out* quotes: "There was no official enquiry." There was certainly no attempt to ask for the black prisoner's side of the story. And why should they? Prisoners are like so many cattle to be dealt with as cattle. Why should anybody ask them their views even if it concerns their liberty and their human rights? This is another blatant example of the contempt and arrogance that characterises they way in which some members of the British Legal Profession deal with prisoner's rights!

My letter of 10th October must have crossed with the President's but you can see from his letter that there was never any intention on anyone's part to investigate this state of affairs in Birmingham. Anyone who steals another's livelihood and another's human rights is a thief and anyone else who refuses to deal with thieves in their own profession is blatantly failing in his professional duty to the public at large, and that is a form of corruption of the public estate.

Phillip Cox wrote to me on the 12th October apparently acknowledging receiving either a copy of my letter that I had sent to him or a copy that Jonas had sent him secretly.

And then on 13th October, 1978, Cox writes to confirm his earlier verbal request for the PCC to see my letter, the very copy that I had sent to the Chairman which nobody ever over the previous period had found objectionable.

The PCC then, after Cox's receiving and writing private letters and by Cox sending his Deputy to the PCC meeting, now the plot has been fully brought together and the machinery and the might of the British legal establishment is set in motion.

On 11th October and even in their letter of 17th October, all the PCC had was my copy of my letter which I had sent them and a verbal message from Cox. These men were so determined to get me that they couldn't even wait for a formal letter of complaint from Cox. They actually decided against me without having a document of complaint before them! Another piece of news that I imagine the public would never believe about the legal profession of England. This decision, I regret to record for historical purposes only, was taken by a committee presided over by a Chairman who should know better.

You will see my response in my letter of 18th October and I stand by what I said then.

You will note that the Chairman of the Bar Council caused the Deputy Secretary of the Senate to write to me to say that the Bar could not deal with my complaints. Phillip Cox had said to me in his letter of 12th October that the Bar could not investigate the conduct of solicitors, so it is totally clear that no machinery exists with the Bar for the investigation of my complaints. This is an important point since if solicitors are breaking their own professional rules at any cost and against the rights of prisoners who can I turn to if my own profession cannot or will not investigate? But I do not accept that they cannot investigate these matters in the Bar Council. They can and they should and they must. The Bar has a total and professional duty not to allow the Law Society to use its members as prostitutes in the sense of sending unwanted barristers against the wishes of the client.

Since there is apparently no machinery at the Bar to investigate my complaints, where can I turn to?

I have already amply demonstrated the transparent unwillingness of the Birmingham Law Society to investigate. So perhaps I can complain to the Law Society in London.

But no, I cannot even do that. This is what the Secretary of the London HQ of the Law Society wrote to me.

He wrote that he could not deal with my complaints but they might look at them if the prisoners themselves wrote. But I sent them the letters from the prisoners and they sent them back to me without investigating!

So if the Bar and the Law Society will not investigate my complaints, who will? Well, I tried the Commission for Racial Equality. I asked for an official enquiry as long ago as 1973 when I wrote an article in *Westindian World* newspaper calling on the then Race Relations Board to investigate the legal profession. I have complained and asked the CRE over the years to investigate and they will not. I have raised this officially and informally.

Now, if the Bar will not investigate, if the Law Society will not investigate, if the CRE will not investigate who can I turn to?

I have complained in newspapers, I have complained on television, I have complained to the Bar Council, I have complained to the Law Society, I have complained to the CRE. Everyone including the black Bar and groups like the NCCL and the Bar and the Law Society themselves know I speak the truth and I always shall. Yet instead of putting their house in order they seek my crucifixion this Easter time. As far as crucifixions go I say here before the Bar of the Common People and before the Bar of History that, despite the cowardice of the barristers who could, if they wished, stand up and fight with the evidence of truth here today and if only the NCCL, Amnesty International, Justice and The Society of Labour Lawyers, if they would only come here today and speak the truth it would not be just one man's life at stake, it would be the betterment of the quality of Justice for years to come. But I do not shrink from this crucifixion; if I have to be extended for this cause then my life is yours; if I have to be harassed and hounded now so that other barristers may benefit from the flowers that spring around my professional grave, then I welcome the sharp blade of Injustice, I do not shrink from it.

But the point that I make is this. If I cannot take my complaints to my professional bodies or to institutions set up to remedy racial injustice what then is my last resort? Only the public is left to me and that is why I say: I was forced to go public, I had to, it was a matter affecting the public and whenever professional bodies act against the public interest then it is the highest duty of the members of that profession to turn to the citizens most affected by such degenerate and illegal professional practices.

Incidentally, for the record, the Law Society's official attitude to this question of the client's right of choice is stated thus: "The choice of counsel is one for the client."

That has always been so but what is happening is this, the rich man can fire and hire as he wishes. But the poor man and the black man and the man in prison, manacled to a firm of solicitors by a legal aid certificate, gets whatever counsel the solicitors foist on him. So that it is one law for the rich and one for the poor. I state here today emphatically: The field of human rights does not admit of discrimination on grounds of race, colour, creed or poverty.

To every man is given certain human rights and from these rights of a poor man, of a man in trouble, of a man facing loss of liberty, of a man locked up behind prison bars, he who takes away one shred of that man's rights is a thief and any solicitor in England who does so is acting unprofessionally.

You will see my letter of 3rd December and I stand by that.

Now I was informed that the PCC was going to charge me on the 3rd January, 1979.

This meeting at which the decision to charge me was taken followed my speech at the AGM of the Bar in December, 1978, when I again attacked the Bar openly for dealing in a racist way with this particular matter, so I am in no doubt about this. I have shown the dishonesty and the dealing in lies and deception by people in the highest places in the legal profession.

I have stated my reasons for being vigorous and going public.

I say that all that I did was in the public interest, all that I did was in the interests of the profession, all that I did was for the good of all people both black and white.

Now, in the presence of the black communities of England

assembled here today from Leeds, Manchester, Birmingham, Cardiff, Southampton, Bristol, Brixton and Notting Hill, not one single barrister has dared to attend here today and speak out publicly about what they know is the truth.

They are scared of *you*.

I am not.

I never have been.

I do not need to be.

I am not a dishonest barrister nor am I an incompetent one.

I am perhaps one of the men the Bar of England should be proud of.

I have done nothing wrong.

I have simply stood up and exercised my freedom of speech as a full citizen of a free and democratic society.

Every citizen has a right to protest and being a barrister cannot take away my rights as a citizen.

I have stood up and exposed a state of affairs that should be exposed. You should really give me a medal.

I have done this vigorously and boldly. Much good will accrue to the public and the professions because of what I have done.

I have suffered from loss of livelihood. I have suffered from loss of dignity as a human being. My brothers in the communities and in the prisons up and down this country are suffering, and in this profession.

I would not be much of a barrister if I enjoyed the fruits of my own profession without making some kind of contribution to the black communities of England.

My contribution to them is that I stand up and fight, in every place and against any person.

You must not deny me the right to fight for my brothers and for my people both in and out of Court. If I tell lies to a Court of Law that would be professional misconduct, if I acted without instructions that would be professional misconduct.

If I interfered with the jury that would be professional misconduct.

But just because I tell protest against the evil of discrimination, just because I let the public know what I am doing that's not reason enough for the Bar to bring proceedings against me.

Cannot the Bar of England allow such freedom to protect myself by complaint?

What happened to the England of Free Speech, whatever happened to the duty of a barrister to stand up fearlessly against all injustice whether in or out of Court.

I believe, and I address these words to all those of the Bar of England and Wales who have a strong sense of social justice, I believe that I have done more good by speaking out than to allow the evil to flourish unchecked; to see and not to speak would be weak and cowardly. I am not a candidate for cowardice.

I have done nothing wrong. All that I have done is now before the public and before you.

I am totally proud of what I have done. I know the public and history will acquit me. Knowing that as surely as I do, I seek the same verdict from you.

For all our sakes, I hope you act with Justice!"

(Extracted from *Barrister on Trial*, published November, 1980, by Hansib Pubishing Ltd).

Part III

Narayan before the Scarman Inquiry into
the Brixton Riots, 1981

PART III

The Scarman Inquiry into the Brixton Riots, 1981

"The Scarman Inquiry was, professionally speaking, a most exciting experience. Lord Scarman is not only courteous, he is lightning fast and eminently brilliant with it and keeping up with him was extremely hard work. But it offered wide scope for the technique of cross-examination, knowing that every phrase would be re-echoed around the world or flashed across the nation's television screens." R.N.

The object of the Brixton Defence Campaign (BDC) was to prevent the facts of the cases which were due to be heard before the courts from being canvassed in public before trial and Narayan's cross-examination was also directed by ensuring that Brixton Police were clearly shown up as the true perpetrators of the riots. What follows here are mere excerpts but they are enough to illustrate the technique of cross-examination.

ARIF ALI

Excerpt (1) Cross-examination of Rene Webb

Note: Rene Webb was then, and still is, a highly regarded grass roots leader of Brixton's black communities and, coming late into the Inquiry as BDC did, it was essential first to stamp BDC's own brand of advocacy on the Inquiry (*The Times* called Narayan "dynamic and aggressive" and the *Sunday Times* "flamboyant and precise") and it was also desperately necessary to establish "background" about the conduct of Brixton Police officers in the run-up to the confrontation in the streets. The first six questions of Webb were "setting-the-scene"

questions and were immediately effective in placing Brixton Police
on public trial.   Arif Ali

Q. Mr. Webb, you know that beginning with the Friday night and
moving to Monday morning there were a large number of arrests by
police?

A. Yes.

Q. Do you know that a large number of those arested are yet to
come before the courts?

A. Yes.

Q. You are asked the question, the very first question by my
learned friend Mr. Hazan on behalf of the Commissioner of
Metropolitan Police: "Do you agree that the police must not lead the
black community to believe that they are being harassed?" Do you
remember that?

A. Yes.

Q. When these people, young and old, were coming in to you on the
Saturday morning complaining of the police they were really
complaining of police harassment, on the Saturday morning.

A. Yes. Even a week before the riot there were an unusual number
of black youths complaining. I understand now that it was Swamp
'81. Although somebody said yesterday that it was not directed against
the black community I question this because Lambeth is outnumbered 3:1 white to black and yet the amount of people that were
arrested, as we saw, were similar in number white and black although
the black community is outnumbered 3:1.

Q. What there had been by the Friday night was a build-up of
complaints to you and to other community leaders of continuing
police harassment.

A. Yes.

Q. It was getting worse the longer the week went by.

A. Yes.

Q. It was getting worse the longer that the week went by?

A. Yes.

Q. So that by the time of the Friday night incident, as a result of
those complaints, tensions were running high near the front line.

A. Yes.

Q. You did, in your narrative of events, mention this injured person
who was taken away by police. I think you were told by the local chief
of police at the station that night that in fact officers had radioed for an
ambulance.

A. Yes.

Q. You believed that to be true.

A. Yes.

Q. In actual fact no ambulance ever turned up in Railton Road, did it?

A. This I do not know because the boy had been taken to hospital. I never heard of an ambulance.

LORD SCARMAN: Do you know whether an ambulance turned up that night or not – the Friday night?

A. No, I do not know.

LORD SCARMAN: Mr. Narayan, there will of course be evidence and evidence in detail, about the Friday incident from people who were there.

MR. NARAYAN: My lord, I am grateful.

MR. HAZAN: And of course the tapes show that one was radioed for.

LORD SCARMAN: Do not get too enthusiastic, Mr. Hazan.

MR. HAZAN: I do not want there to be a misunderstanding.

LORD SCARMAN: I know what is coming and it may or may not be true. I wanted to make quite clear that Mr. Webb could not help because he does not know. Mr. Narayan can therefore leave this matter for witnesses who do or should know.

MR. NARAYAN: I am grateful to your lordship for curbing Mr. Hazan's enthusiasm.

MR. HAZAN: I am only trying to inform him what he may not know: at 6.24 there was a message.

MR. NARAYAN: (To the Witness) By the time that the incident was over on the Friday night things had calmed down totally.

A. Yes.

Q. In fact there was no reason for massive police presence after the incident that you could see?

A. I have said that I was amazed that there were so many police at that time – although I was told that there would be more police on the street. However, to me it was not necessary for so many police to be there.

Q. You have dealt with the build up of tension in the week moving forward to the Friday night. Can we move now to the Saturday morning. Saturday morning in Brixton is the busiest time of the week. That is right, is is not?

A. Yes.

Q. People come from all over the place to shop at Brixton's market.

A. Yes.

Q. In fact Saturday morning in Brixton, in that particular area of Railton Road, you hardly have room to swing a cat on Saturday morning.

A. Yes.

Q. Nevertheless there were large numbers of police officers stationed in amongst the shoppers on Saturday morning.

A. Yes.

Q. And there was no trouble going on that anyone could see on that Saturday morning.

A. Not as far as I know.

Q. Therefore there was no obvious reason for police officers in large numbers to be in the heart of Brixton on a Saturday morning.

A. I would say that – not as a policeman.

Q. You were asked by Mr. Hazan about stopping and searching. You would not subscribe to the proposition, would you, that police are simply entitled to stop and search innocent persons?

A. That is the objection coming from innocent black people who have been stopped without any reason and searched without any reason. We have had complaints. I do not think they were so much upset at being stopped and searched but at the way that they were stopped.

Q. According to their complaints it included racial abuse.

A. I do not know what it was.

Q. What I want to get from you at this stage is this. You would agree that officers must stop persons they reasonably suspect of having committed a crime.

A. Yes.

Q. But you would not agree that the police can simply stop a thousand people without lawful cause.

A. No. I have said that there is a terrible danger here that innocent people will be stopped.

LORD SCARMAN: What you are saying, Mr. Webb, is that the policeman has to exercise judgement. He has the power to stop, it is given to him by statute, but he should only do so on the grounds of reasonable suspicion.

A. That is right.

MR. NARAYAN: Therefore, judging from the flood of complaints that you community leaders were receiving by the Friday night incident Swamp '81 was an illegal police operation involving unlawful stopping by people abusing their powers. That was the situation, was it not?

A. Yes. That is statistically shown by the amount of people who were stopped and searched and who were innocent.

Q. The complaints that you were receiving showed, assuming that they were true, that the police were acting illegally and unlawfully in that operation Swamp '81.

A. It was because of those complaints that I even knew about Swamp '81.

LORD SCARMAN: Mr. Narayan, you have put a question of law. Questions of law are for me. Questions of fact are for the witness.

MR. NARAYAN: My Lord, I will try and rephrase it quite suitably. Mr. Webb, from the complaints you were getting the people were objecting to being stopped by officers when they had done nothing wrong against the law. Is that right?

A. We always have these kinds of complaints. However, in that period there were more complaints than usual. People were being stopped when they were innocent and were being searched. They repeatedly said that they objected to the way they were searched and to the way that they were stopped.

Q. By the Saturday morning, bearing in mind those complaints, the numbers of people in Brixton, the number of police in Brixton, really the picture of Railton Road and the market area on Saturday morning, when there was no trouble, was a community under siege by police officers.

A. Yes. What I will say is this, and I have said it before, is that I do not object and will not object to the presence of the police. I do not think that the majority of people objected to the presence of police in areas large or small. What they do object to is the kind of policing. Two policemen can do as much harm as a hundred policemen if they are not doing the job properly.

Q. Taking the absence of trouble on the Saturday morning, and the large number of officers in that crowded market place area of Brixton, what you saw amounted to an invasion of the community. There were people questioning the amount of strangers – the police who were strangers to Brixton. Did I understand you correctly to say this: that the home beat officers, the officers who know people locally, had been taken off the streets on the Friday, the Saturday and the Sunday?

A. No, I did not say that they were taken off. I said they were not there. I looked for them that morning but I did not see any of them. I question it all the time: Why was it that people like these were not called out that morning, because I am very sure that the reaction to them would have been very different to the reaction to police coming from outside who they did not know.

Q. We know that Swamp '81 started on the Wednesday, a couple of days before the Friday. Are you saying this: now that we know when Swamp '81 started that there was no sign of the home beat officers on the Wednesday, Thursday or Friday?

A. I cannot remember whether I saw them. I can only remember that incident over the week-end. I certainly did not see them on

Friday and I certainly did not see them on Saturday. I am certain I did not see them on Sunday either. On those three days I did not see them and I formed the opinion at that time that it would have been much better for the community as a whole if these people, who were well known in the area, were called out. I think that they could have done a lot to ease the situation that week-end.

Q. Bearing in mind the complaints flooding in to you on the Saturday morning of how the police were behaving towards innocent people, it must have crossed your mind that sooner or later people would have to defend themselves against unlawful police action?

A. I think that the mood of this community or of any other community when they are pressed and pressed too far is that they will react. There are times, without question – and again I am not judging the whole police force – when there are policemen, and if it is that they are formed from a racist society, then we have got to expect that police like this exist, and it is police like this who create problems, not only for the rest of the police but for the community as a whole.

LORD SCARMAN: Mr. Narayan, I just want to make this clear. Are you suggesting that in such a situation it is likely that people will resort to lawlessness, or are you suggesting that they are justified in doing so?

MR. NARAYAN: Let me phrase it more precisely, my Lord. What I am suggesting to you, Mr. Webb, is this. By the time the flood of complaints was coming in on that Saturday morning, it must have occurred to you that sooner or later people might have to act lawfully in self-defence ...

LORD SCARMAN: Mr. Narayan, it is the words "have to" that I object to in that question. If, of course, you are suggesting it is likely, also say so but make quite clear what you are suggesting.

MR. NARAYAN: My Lord, that is why I am using the word "lawful". Mr. Webb, are you saying they would have to act to defend themselves against unlawful police plunder?

A. I think in any society, when people are really pressed to a point, the danger is there that they will react.

Q. Not only that, but you know of course that the West Indian temperament is a volatile temperament?

A. Yes.

Q. You know that the English Policeman's temperament can be coldly clinical?

LORD SCARMAN: Mr. Narayan, those are generalisations and will not help me to make a valuable report.

MR. NARAYAN: My Lord, I will withdraw that. Mr. Webb, taking it in this way, taking the police presence on the Saturday

morning and the complaints, what was happening there was that
tension was being created, not only by the numbers of police at a
peaceful time but by the way in which they were behaving towards the
people. They were creating the tension, not the people?

A. Yes, I have said that in a community such as this policemen will
have to become fully conversant with the community that they police.
A black guy will react in a certain way that a white guy would not react
in. A Jamaican would react in a certain way that an Englishman would
not react, and these are important things a policeman in this area will
have to know. As a matter of fact, I have walked down the street many
a time and there have been two black guys talking, and if I had not
known what was happening I would have thought they were about to
fight. These are things the police in this area will have to know. I have
criticised the time limit set to educate policemen with such ideas. This
might come out, but I do not think that six months is enough to take a
man from Cornwall and put him in at Hendon, train him for six weeks
or twelve weeks and then put him into Brixton. You have got to
become more conversant with the community.

Q. You were asked about Commander Adams' helpful attitude.
You know, of course, that the Lambeth Borough Council had a
Working Party into Community Relations in Lambeth and that they
published a report?

A. Yes.

Q. Do you know that, in fact, Commander Adams, when asked
about the Special Patrol Group in Brixton said this, bearing in mind
all the officers on the Saturday morning in Brixton: "No good general
ever declares his forces in a prelude to any kind of attack." Do you
know he said that?

A. Yes.

Q. Was that Commander Adams' attitude as you know it; that in
fact he was a general in charge of troops who might need to attack
something in Brixton?

A. In my discussion with Commander Adams and other senior
officers, the things we discussed and the points he raised with me were
pretty fair, and I do not condemn him for this. What I do say is that
there were certain things told to us by that Committee which were not
getting through to the people who were policing the streets. The
problem here, without any question, is that we have a lot of young
policemen. I do not object to people being young because I was young
once, but I think young policemen are quicker to react to certain
things than older policemen. I think this is a problem for the whole
country, because where do we get those kind of numbers to police the
streets? I think that young policemen are much quicker to react to

certain things than old policemen.

Q. You mentioned that you were a bit more concerned than usual because on the Saturday morning it was not just the youths complaining but, in fact, black adults as well. You said that caused you even more concern?

A. Yes, that is true. Although older blacks have always been coming to us for advice, most of them have never complained about police harassment. It was over this weekend, where adult blacks were coming and complaining about police harassment, when I was really alerted to certain things. I was terribly upset with it and I was terribly concerned about it because here was a group of people who did not usually complain about harassment of the police, and they were doing this now.

Q. Really, on the Saturday morning, black people of all ages were complaining of police conduct?

A. Yes, they were. I think some of the complaints were that the youth was arrested overnight and they did not know where he was. We tried desperately to find out from Brixton but they were not in a position to tell us. That, again, I could sympathise with because it is such a terrible problem. They did not know where he was.

Q. In a street situation where there are large numbers of police and large numbers of people, you can I suppose sometimes detect whether the police are bent on cooling things down on the one hand, or seeking to confront people violently on the other?

A. Yes.

Q. From what you saw, especially bearing in mind the incident you saw in Saltoun Road with the officers marching – by the way, were they marching or walking?

A. Some were running, I think, and some were walking.

Q. Were they in a military formation?

A. Well, that incident that I saw in Saltoun Road . . .

Q. Were they in a military formation bearing shields which makes His Lordship think back to Roman times?

A. Yes. They were coming down with shields.

Q. In that manner of aggression?

A. Yes.

Q. And they were attacking an empty street at the time?

A. Well, as I said, when they came down that street there was nobody about. It was an empty street I spoke about.

Q. From the way you saw police with shields and the way they were behaving Mr. Webb, as a senior experienced member of the Brixton community were they in fact seeking to cool things down or were they bent on crushing everybody in sight?

A. I have already said that there are certain policemen who are not concerned with community relations. All they are concerned about is arresting people – yes, I have said that.

Q. Were they seeking to confront and overcome by physical means, as opposed to cooling things down?

A. Yes, a section of the police were behaving like that.

Q. Of course, seeing police moving in formation and number, what was happening was this, that people were not moving in numbers and formation they were simply moving in ones and twos?

A. Yes.

Q. But the police were moving in large organised groups?

A. Well, it depends upon the period you are talking about. Certainly that Saturday night, at the height of the riot, people were moving about. The incident I talk about on the Sunday, the empty street with nobody there, the police came down in formation with their shields and I thought at this time that they had made a terrible mistake in doing things like this.

LORD SCARMAN: Mr. Webb, as I understand it, when you came back that Saturday afternoon, rather late really, and saw the situation had deteriorated, the total situation included premises and other property being burnt and some groups of young people down Railton Road and the police in an organised formation also in Railton Road?

A. Yes.

Q. Of course, there were some people moving about in ones and twos?

A. Yes.

Q. But there was also a group of persons down Railton Road where the fires and damage were?

A. Yes.

MR. NARAYAN: But bearing in mind that Saltoun Road marching, the police advancing on the empty street, at the time they were advancing in the way you have told us in Saltoun Road there was no looting or burning in front of the advancing officers, was there? It was simply a peaceful empty street?

A. Yes, there was nobody there.

Q. Really, taking it all together – what you saw and the complaints – did it occur to you at the end of it, looking back at all the complaints you had, the build up, the numbers, the officers, what you saw them do, that in fact the last thing the police had on their minds was conciliation with the community?

A. Well, I think that this riot did not come about by outside help, and it suddenly stopped. These people vented their feelings and it stopped. I think in the days the police were in the area, without any question, I knew by talking to people again that at least now this was the end of the riot. I think the police were not sure that this was the end of it.

LORD SCARMAN: Mr. Webb, I am not quite sure about this. Were you present when missiles and petrol bombs were being thrown?

A. Yes.

Q. Do you understand that there are difficulties about a conciliation effort when missiles and petrol bombs are being thrown?

A. I understand that quite well, sir. That is why I said I am more interested in the cause of the riot than the riot itself. When there is a riot then we are going to have missiles, and maybe at some point it will be uncontrollable. Certainly that night I was turned back by the police twice but I tried to get through, and it was very hard for me to get through. There was a terrible confrontation taking place between the police and youths.

MR. NARAYAN: Pursuing His Lordship's question further, the area of the petrol bombs being thrown, as I understand it, is that area of Railton Road where the triangle begins and moving up Railton Road?

A. Yes, I think that was part of it – Leeson Road.

Q. But even before petrol bombs were thrown, police were already behaving in a hostile and aggressive manner towards the people?

A. I have said before that in the week leading up to the riot there was a lot of hostility by the police. That is according to what was told to me. I was told that young policemen in plain clothes were harassing them on Railton Road, were stepping on their feet and things like that, and pushing them about.

LORD SCARMAN: On the Saturday you came to the riot when, unfortunately, it was well developed. You did not get there until quite late in the afternoon.

A. That is right.

MR. NARAYAN: The last area I seek your assistance on is this. You know, of course, that arrests took place into the following week, the Monday/Tuesday?

A. Yes.

Q. Did you get complaints into the following week of the way in which police officers visited homes in that area?

A. We are getting complaints; complaints are still coming in of police going into people's houses.

Q. Did the complaints of police visits to homes, after that weekend, include complaints of brutality and breaking down doors?

A. We are getting complaints like that. I have to verify them, but I have had those complaints, yes.

Q. I want now to find out this from you. We can say events cooled down generally on the Monday. We are now moving into the Tuesday/Wednesday/Thursday following. Were there complaints in that following week of police officers breaking down doors?

A. We are still getting complaints.

Q. Even now?

A. That last complaint I had was last Tuesday. I have not been able to verify it, but we had a lot of complaints after the riot and we are still having complaints.

Q. Leaving aside breaking down doors, did you get complaints of officers beating up people when they visited their homes to arrest them?

A. The beating I heard about was during the riot. I know a family who complained that the police came into their house.

Q. Is that Mr. Swabey?

A. I do not want to quote names, but police came into his house and his hand was broken.

Q. How recent, according to your complaints because you say you have had some recently, have these police visitations been? Have they been in the last week or two to these homes, according to your complaints?

A. I had complaints up to last Tuesday that police went into homes not far from Railton Road. It was about things that happened in the riots.

Q. The complaints date back to the weekend of the riots, do they?

A. They are doing it now because of what happened in the riots.

Q. The police officers in Brixton, even now, according to your complaints, are visiting homes in Brixton and behaving badly?

A. According to the complaints I have heard, yes.

Q. Even now, right up to now?

A. That last one I had was last Tuesday, I said.

The Scarman Inquiry into the Brixton Riots, 1981.

(2) The Cross-examination of Councillor Ted Knight, Leader of Lambeth Council.

NOTE:

The cross-examination of Councillor Ted Knight had two objectives. The first was to throw him a credibility lifebelt after his cross-examination by John Hazan QC, now Judge Hazan QC, Counsel for the Police. But the second, more important reason, was to establish Brixton Police stupidity and stubbornness in the face of democratically elected people warning them of flashing red lights. It was absolutely necessary for the Press and public to see how aggressively and ignorantly the police had behaved and Narayan's first fifteen questions set Knight up for the rescue of the "law and order" question to allow him the chance to recover from Hazan's attack. The rest is thorough establishing of "background."

Arif Ali

Q. You have been asked about law and order on the streets by my learned friend Mr. Hazan for the police. When you saw policemen apparently hitting a man who had been dragged off his bike, is that the kind of law and order you support?

A. No.

Q. Earlier, and just to indicate the time and date precisely, you indicated that you were in Brixton Town Hall at about 8.30 pm on the Saturday evening. Is that right?

A. Yes, that would be about the time I got to Brixton Town Hall.

Q. You indicated that large numbers of people, both black and white, and including children, were walking up and down Brixton Road?

Q. That is right.

I think you mentioned the word "families"?

A. Yes.

Q. At that time you said there were no police officers actually in that part of Brixton Road?

A. That is correct.

Q. So the situation was that whatever had happened previously to shops it was then a peaceful scene?

A. It was a peaceful scene, yes.

Q. A peaceful scene including women and children?

A. Yes, it looked like families in total. In other words, complete families were out on the streets.

LORD SCARMAN: It was a strange thing, was it not?

A. It was yes.

Q. It was peaceful. It was a warm evening and here were families out strolling, and yet behind them there were broken shops and every now and then people going in and out of those shops, possibly looting?

A. Yes, it was a very strange scene, not one I had witnessed in Brixton before.

Q. I have, in fact, witnessed before, and it is a very strange thing.

A. Yes it is. Somebody has mentioned a carnival and that was a misuse really of terms, but it was a strange atmosphere, yes.

LORD SCARMAN: If you know Belfast and Londonderry you will have seen this sort of situation.

MR NARAYAN: But although it was a strange scene, it was a peaceful scene?

A. Yes.

Q. There was no-one at that time that you could see committing crimes?

A. Not at all, no, and I was able, as obviously everybody else was, to walk along the streets without any problem.

Q. That applies to both black and white?

A. Yes, absolutely.

Q. It was on to that peaceful scene that this police van drove into the wrong side of Brixton Road?

A. Yes, it was on several occasions.

Q. It was into that peaceful scene that police officers emerged from the van and this happened five times I think you said?

A. I estimated it to be five times, yes.

Q. As they emerged, they would jump out and run into the crowd with truncheons in their hands?

A. Yes.

Q. At the time that these officers would jump out and run into the crowd with truncheons drawn, could you see anyone creating any trouble?

A. No, not at all.

Q. So that as regards the law and order that Mr Hazan invited you to contemplate, is that the kind of law and order you support – police officers in a peaceful scene jumping out and running about with truncheons drawn?

A. No, it is not.

Q. Later – and I would like to get the time from you please in a moment – you were in the Town Hall overlooking that angle of Brixton between the Orange Coach Station on the right and the Prince of Wales?

A. Yes.

Q. That covers the front, of course, of the library frontage – the open space?

A. Yes, you can see that.

Q. So that covers something, I would have thought, in the region of 400 yards?

A. I would think it must, yes.

Q. Would this be after 9.30?

A. Yes, it would be.

Q. How long after 9.30 would this be, when you are standing looking out?

A. I estimated it, on reflection, to be about an hour or an hour and a half afterwards.

Q. So it could be going on to elevenish?

A. I would have thought it was approximately 11 o'clock.

Q. At that time, as you looked out, you described the earlier peaceful scene in Brixton Road, when you were first there. Now, as you are looking out through the window, again you see the police sorties into Brixton Road?

A. Yes.

Q. At that time in Brixton Road, as you looked out, did you see any persons breaking the laws? We will come to the police in a moment.

A. No, I could not see from where I was standing, looking out the window, anyone breaking the law.

LORD SCARMAN: Mr Knight, you have been very fair about all these matters. It is difficult at a distance to see either the beginning of an incident or, indeed, what its cause is. You see the incident and you may see its conclusion?

A. Yes, I think that is a very valid point.

MR NARAYAN: Let me put it more specifically than that then. Did you see anyone from where you were standing throwing stones?

A. No, I did not see anyone doing that.

Q. I think you numbered the earlier police sorties with truncheons drawn as five?

A. Yes, that was from a van. They were jumping out of a van.

Q. Can you number the sorties, roughly, that you are now looking out on to?

A. It was happening regularly. In other words, it was a continuous movement of police moving into crowds and moving back from them, so I could not number them so it was a sort of regular feature.

Q. Did these officers leave in groups of two or three or four or what?

A. No, they were in larger numbers than that.

Q. Moving together?

A. Yes, as a sort of large group moving.

Q. A sort of squad?

A. I would use that term probably myself without knowing quite how it defines.

Q. Did these policemen, now that you are looking out through the window, have truncheons drawn as well?

A. Some did and others not. In other words, we saw them running sometimes with truncheons drawn and other times not.

Q. When they were running, were they in fact running at people standing on the pavement?

A. That was the impression one got, yes. They were running and one was attracted, of course, by their movements and then they were moving in a crowd of people.

Q. As they moved into the crowd of people, would they do this: run up in a group, as a squad, some truncheons drawn, and push those people physically through Brixton Road?

A. That would appear to be what was happening, but of course the angle of vision is not such that you could see how it continued.

Q. What I am trying to get at is this. Were the people they were moving towards simply people standing or walking around?

A. Yes. My understanding of it was that crowds were gathering in Brixton Road. They were there when I was there and they tended to continue to be there. It appears to be a process of moving such crowds in various directions.

Q. Of course, that area – correct me if I am wrong – was cordoned off from traffic?

A. Yes, it was cordoned off.

Q. So although there were a large number of people there, they were obstructing – if they were – a cordoned off street through which no traffic was passing?

A. Yes; they certainly were not holding up the traffic.

Q. So what the police were doing really was trying to move away essentially peaceful crowds?

A. That was certainly my view, and from the physical appearance of it, yes.

Q. Peaceful crowds that included women and children?

A. Oh, there certainly were children present and there were certainly women.

Q. In this situation that you then saw, the aggression that you could see came from the police against peaceful citizens?

A. Well, certainly I saw that in their excursions from the van. It certainly appeared that that may have continued. Physically that was the appearance I was seeing.

Q. May I invite your attention again to the Orange Coach Station. This is the incident with the black man outside the Orange Coach Station. Had you seen or taken notice of him before he was grabbed by police?

A. No, what attracted me was the movement of the police.

Q. When they grabbed him, was it one officer, two, three or what happened?

A. My memory of the situation is that it was some three or four policemen who actually grabbed him. They then took him out of our vision, or my vision. I was also there with other colleagues.

Q. When you say "grabbed" do you mean "grabbed"?

A. Yes, I mean physically grabbed hold of my clothing and other means.

Q. Did they invite him gently round the back, or did they drag him there?

A. It appeared that he moved without his own intention.

LORD SCARMAN: They seized him, did they not?

A. I think that is a better term, yes. Seizing, grabbing, I think it is probably a better term.

MR. NARAYAN: You have referred to the flashes of light. That could be a photographer's camera bulb going off?

A. It could be. I believe it to be such. At first I was not clear what it was, but I since have seen reports that tend to confirm that.

Q. Was that man on the motor-bike rushed on by three or four policemen?

A. Yes, he was.

Q. Did they physically drag him off his bike?

A. Yes.

Q. You have been very fair in saying that they appeared to be kicking him, but let us put it this way – were the policemen's legs moving in his direction as he lay on the ground?

A. There was an activity among standing people that would have indicated that, yes. In other words, certainly they looked as if they were moving but they were not...

LORD SCARMAN: Mr. Knight, about how far away were you from them?

A. It is the distance from the Town Hall to the pavement of the road opposite, outside the Orange Station. It is a fair distance.

Q. That is looking across the open land to the north of St. Matthew's Church?

A. Yes, one can just miss the trees and the other things.

LORD SCARMAN: Yes, I know exactly the viewpoint now.

MR. NARAYAN: From what you could see, did you then believe they were kicking him?

A. Yes, I came to that conclusion immediately.

Q. You have been asked a number of questions by Mr. Blom-Cooper and Mr. Hazan. I wish to see if we can clarify some of those questions and answers. My Lord, might I ask formally whether this Report might be exhibited to the Inquiry?

LORD SCARMAN: It is already an exhibit. Mr. Narayan, if you are passing now to a new point I think this would be a convenient moment to adjourn.

(Adjourned for a short time)

Q. I want to pursue the clarification of matters which were raised by Mr. Blom-Cooper and Mr. Hazan, and the first question I want to ask you is this: you were asked a lot of questions about the Inquiry that produced the Final Report of the Working Party into Community/Police Relations in Lambeth published in January, 1981. You, of course, are leader of the majority party in the Council, are you not?

A. Yes.

Q. But we notice that the minority party was represented by a councillor being on the Working Party. Is that right?

A. Yes, that is correct.

Q. Does that mean that the minority party agreed with the setting up of this Inquiry?

A. Yes, I would have taken that to be agreement, certainly. They were prepared to nominate one of their persons to serve on the Working Party.

Q. Otherwise, if they did not agree , you would expect them not to participate?

A. Yes.

Q. The other matter is the private meeting at Brixton Police Station, it was suggested to you that Mr. Shelton, MP, disagreed with the Inquiry. Of course, there were three other MPs there, were there not?

A. Yes. There was Mr. John Fraser, Mr. John Tilley and, I believe,

Mr. Stuart Holland was also there.

Q. And those three MPs I take it agreed with the Inquiry?

A. Yes. They expressed no opposition about it to me.

Q. It was also put to you that Mr. Laws disagreed, but were there other community people there apart from Mr. Laws?

A. As I recall it, there were. I frankly cannot remember who was present. It was not a recorded meeting as such.

Q. We know it was recorded by the police if not by you?

A. I did not think there was a need for such a record to be made.

Q. When the Inquiry was set up we notice that chairing the Inquiry was someone as distinguished as Mr. Blom-Cooper and Mr. Hazan, Mr. Turner-Samuels, QC?

A. Yes. It was our intention to approach and to secure the services of a QC gentleman or lady who would be respected in their profession.

Q. Also on the Inquiry was the Chairperson of the Council for Community Relations in Lambeth?

A. Yes.

Q. And a representative of Lambeth Trades Council?

A. Yes.

Q. The Borough Dean of Lambeth, Canon Pinder?

A. Yes.

Q. A distinguished writer, Amrit Wilson?

A. Yes.

Q. And then the minority representative, Councillor Bays?

A. Yes.

Q. And two other councillors, Bowring and Griffiths. Then a representative from Hammersmith Council for Community Relations?

A. Yes.

Q. So that really, looking at the set-up of the Inquiry personnel, it was a cross-section of persons and interested parties across the community?

A. That was certainly my view and I think the view generally of the Council.

Q. Once this inquiry was set up and the personnel appointed and the Chairmanship allocated, was there anything that you or any other person could do to interfere with its working?

A. I think it would have been very difficult to have attempted to do so, because we had said that the Working Party would have independence of the Council and any other influences, and certainly it would not be my intention nor the intention I think of any elected member to have interfered.

LORD SCARMAN: Put shortly, you did not do so and it is their Report?

A. Thank you.

MR. NARAYAN: It follows that it is their Report, but all the wording, headings, headlines and everything in this Report, come from them and not from you or any member of the Council?

A. That is true.

Q. If we look at the headline at which you were invited to look on page 6, "Army of Occupation", you will see that just under that title there is a quote from Commander Adams. This is what he said apparently on television: "No good General ever declares his forces in a prelude to any kind of attack." Do you see that?

A. Yes.

Q. So that there was a Commander Adams, presupposing himself as a General in charge of troops, referring to an attack?

A. That certainly is my reading of it.

Q. So that leaving aside the quotation, do you see below there that from 1975 to 1979, there were six attacks by the SPG on the people of Lambeth and also references to road blocks, early morning raids and random street checks?

A. That was certainly the experience of those periods, yes.

Q. So that the military phrasing or certainly part of it comes from Commander Adams himself?

A. Yes. I read that to be the case, certainly.

Q. You were asked about whether or not the police were invited to participate and when they were. If you look at page 93 of the Report do you see that, although it was announced back in March, the Working Party held its first meeting on 28th August, 1979?

A. Yes.

Q. If you now turn to page 96, there is the letter from the Chairman to the local Commander within 20 days of the first meeting of the Working Party?

A. Yes, that certainly is the position.

Q. Of course, that invitation to the Commander could only have been extended, speaking in terms of democracy and logicality, by the Chairman?

A. That is quite the case. Certainly it would not have been extended by me on behalf of the Chairman.

Q. If you take that letter on page 96 together with the Chairman's second letter to Commander Adams on page 98, you will see that in fact two separate invitations were issued by the Chairman.

A. Yes, I am aware of that.

Q. If you look at the reply on page 97 from Mr Adams, while that is of some length, if you look at page 99 the offer of the Chairman to meet the local Commander is simply dismissed in about two lines. Do you see that?

A. Yes. It certainly does not explain the position at any length.

Q. You were asked about accountability both by learned counsel and by his lordship. As leader of the Council you would know that Lambeth Council of course lawfully levies rates on rate-payers in the Borough?

A. I am aware of that, yes.

Q. And part of the rates that are levied by the Council that you lead goes towards the police?

A. Yes, they do. A percentage of it goes towards the police. It is called a precept.

Q. Am I right in this: that the money goes from Lambeth Council to the GLC?

A. It certainly goes to the police. Whether it goes via the GLC, I do not know.

Q. Do you know how much money a year of ratepayers' money from Lambeth goes towards the police, just roughly?

A. I cannot give an off-the-cuff answer to that.

Q. Would it be something in excess of half a million pounds?

LORD SCARMAN: I do not think you need to spend time, Mr. Knight. You can arrange for those who are advising you to let me have that figure?

A. Yes, certainly. It is a large sum of money.

MR. NARAYAN: The money that is taken from the ratepayers of Lambeth and ratepayers in other Boroughs goes towards paying all expenses of keeping a police force in London?

A. Yes, it is shared between the Boroughs of London.

Q. It pays for their salaries and equipment, and the whole lot?

A. Yes.

Q. For example, if there is a massive demonstration that the police have to protect or guard, that comes from comes the ratepayers' money?

A. Yes, it certainly would. If they were running at a deficit as a consequence, there would be an increase in the precept the following year.

Q. So that the same people who pay rates in Lambeth are, by definition, the people that the police are employed to protect?

A. Yes, every ratepayer is paying towards the cost of the police in Lambeth and elsewhere.

Q. You of course have been a resident of Lambeth, you have been a councillor for Lambeth, and you are now Leader of the Lambeth

Council. You were asked about accountability. Would you, for example, like to see black people on Police Complaints Boards?

A. I certainly would . I would like to see that. I would like to see Police Complaints Boards and the police complaints procedure made open to the public in every way.

LORD SCARMAN: You would like to see black men in the Police Force, would you not?

A. I think that a multi-racial population should be reflected at all levels.

MR. NARAYAN: In fact, where complaints are made against the police involving a significant number of black people complaining, would it be useful and democratic to have black people sitting in judgement of police officers?

A. I think there is no question about that.

Q. Just stopping there on the word "Complaints", would you turn to page 80 of the Report. It begins with the words, "A Home Office Research Bulletin published at the end of 1979 for 1978 included a study which showed that not a single complaint against the police was upheld by the Metropolitan Police complaints procedure in the years 1973 to 1978." Bearing that in mind, is there an important argument for participation by those who pay the police to be sitting in judgement on their conduct?

A. I think it is the old adage: Why payment, yet no representation? I think that is very true.

Q. When complaints are made against the conduct of local officers are a large number of those complaints made to local councillors?

A. Local councillors find themselves faced with complaints by residents but probably not as many as would our Members of Parliament.

Q. This Inquiry that was set up, was it set up as far as you know, after a build up of tension in Lambeth?

A. It certainly was.

Q. Was that build up of tension, as far as you could see, largely attributable to police conduct against the citizens of Lambeth?

A. That certainly was my view. I think it also was the view of the Council that relationships between the police and the community in general had reached such a low level that it was essential that there should be an investigation to see what the causes of that situation were.

Q. In the public interest?

A. We were acting, as a Council, with the public interest at heart – without doubt. I think that Councillors were well aware from the complaints that they were receiving what the problems were. I might add that the Conservative Member of Parliament for Streatham ...

LORD SCARMAN: Mr. Knight, I have assumed that you believed that you were acting in the public interest. There is no doubt about that. Mr. Narayan, a number of these questions are not so much directed to persuading me of facts of which I am well aware as parading certain views in public.

MR. NARAYAN: The problem is that Your Lordship allowed questions to the contrary to be asked ...

LORD SCARMAN: I have not objected to the question. I think that there is always a danger of taking these things too far.

MR. NARAYAN: I am anxious to deal with the situation created by questions asked by two of my learned friends earlier.

LORD SCARMAN: The use of the adjective "democratic" after "useful" adds nothing to my thinking. It merely adds a political dimension to what you and I know, and what Mr. Knight has been careful to observe, it is a non-political Inquiry.

MR. NARAYAN: I shall try to avoid the use of the word "democratic". (To the Witness): Leaving yourself personally aside was it clear to you that the entire Lambeth Council, including majority and minority parties, were anxious to avoid an explosion in Lambeth similar to that which occurred in Bristol?

A. I think that that applied to every member of the Council.

Q. When the debates were in session in the Council Chamber to discuss the setting up of the Inquiry was Bristol in fact mentioned as part of that debate?

A. It was. It would have been impossible to have discussed the situation that we were experiencing in Lambeth without making reference to Bristol.

Q. The other matter is this. You were asked by his Lordship earlier about stopping and searching.

A. Yes.

Q. I am sure that you would agree, and we would all agree, that stopping and searching on reasonable grounds, such as stopping a criminal or thief, is reasonable.

A. Yes.

Q. Take these figures – not the one that the Tribunal has had earlier – new figures. In that five days of Swamp '81 in Lambeth, 2,089 people were stopped; 118 were arrested and 79 were charged. If you accept those figures 2,010 innocent citizens were stopped by police in Brixton in five days.

A. In actual fact I was appalled at the previous figures which would have indicated something over a thousand such people.

Q. That is right. Taking that situation, 2000 innocent citizens, some of them ratepayers, stopped during five days in Brixton, perhaps the heart of Brixton, if you wanted to start a riot in Brixton it was one way of going about it. That is right, is it not?

A. I did bring this to the attention of Commander Fairbairn. It was not productive.

Q. It comes to this: that in the build up of police conduct in the community over the previous month, before the weekend of 10th to 11th April, the situation that you could see was building up to a situation where the community could not survive police activities of that kind?

A. I was not alone in this. It came from discussions with colleagues and discussions that were held in the Council Chamber itself. All Councillors were concerned from the response that they were receiving at their surgeries, advice bureaux and letters that they were receiving, that there was a massive build up of tension within the area. This was confirmed also by discussions which I had as leader of the Council with Members of Parliament.

Q. Was the situation this: it was building up to an explosion point and one way of dealing with it was to have this Public Inquiry as fast as you could possibly arrange it?

A. We thought that that was absolutely necessary. When the suggestion came before the Council we felt that this was a worthwhile operation – to avail the Council of the facts. That is why we took the decision. We hoped to try before too late to learn some lessons and to gain understanding of facts we were not fully aware of.

Q. Please look at page 4 of the report. The third quotation down reads as follows: "The community may not survive this kind of policing." Do you see that?

A. Yes.

Q. Was that the situation as you understand it to be when this Inquiry was set up – that the community could not survive that kind of policing?

A. Yes. I think that that was very clearly our view.

Q. You have been asked about the question of burglaries and robberies. My Lord, would you give me permission to consult a note?

LORD SCARMAN: Yes.

MR. NARAYAN: My Lord, I will have to leave this point. If I get the information from the police may I return to it again?

LORD SCARMAN: Certainly, Mr. Narayan.

MR. NARAYAN: I did ask Councillor Knight if he was aware of the money paid out of rates towards the upkeep of the police. Estimates handed to me now by the representative of Lambeth Borough Council show that in 1980 it was £6 million; 1980 to 1981 –

£7.5 million; 1981 to 1982 – £8.8 million from Lambeth to the Metropolitan Police. Bearing in mind that that amount of money came from the pockets of the ratepayers of Lambeth have the police shown any interest in consulting elected representatives of the people?

A. I do not consider that there has been such an interest. I do not consider that one visit to discuss it formally is consulting elected members.

MR. NARAYAN: My Lord, subject to that one point I have no further questions.

LORD SCARMAN: If Mr. Knight is not here you may be able to get the point from somebody else.

MR. NARAYAN: I am grateful to Your Lordship. Thank you, Mr. Knight.

The Scarman Inquiry into the Brixton Riots, 1981

(3) The Cross-Examination of P.C. John Brown

NOTE:

This cross-examination was a friendly one since its whole intention was to establish that black people would, could and did respond with courtesy to decent, law-abiding police officers. John Brown was then and still is one of the nicest persons in uniform and this cross-examination, building him up as it did, drew lots of jealousy and resentment from some others at Brixton Police Station. This cross-examination also let out the ropes a bit and gave the Press the chance to do some lovely cameo articles on John Brown. Watch for the questions about "pretty-as-a-picture on a Saturday morning" Brixton. Painting in words but with a very light brush.

Arif Ali

Q. Mr. Brown, I think you are extremely well known in the Railton Road area, are you not?

A. Yes, I am.

Q. I am not clear myself about the number of years you have spent as home beat officer on that beat?

A. Since 1971.

Q. So it is 10 years.

A. Yes.

Q. As home beat officer for that precise area?

A. Yes.

Q. And during those 10 years you visit schools, do you?

A. Yes.

Q. Youth clubs?

A. Yes.

Q. Old age pensioner clubs?

A. Yes.

Q. You are known at the Melting Pot, are you?

A. Yes.

Q. You were known at the Brixton Neighbourhood?

A. Yes.

Q. The Methodist Church in Railton Road; were you known there?

A. Yes.

Q. And really what you do is to try and cover physically by visiting almost every single organised club in the area?

A. Yes, I do.

Q. Not limiting it to black or white, but people of all races?

A. That is right.

Q. And not limiting it to youths; you also visit the infants' play group and the old age pensioners and everything in between?

A. That is right.

Q. So what you do by physically visiting is that you cover physically as much of the people in those clubs as you can?

A. That is correct.

Q. Obviously you cannot go into people's homes, but wherever people gather in an organised fashion that is where you go?

A. Yes.

Q. And you do it nearly every day when you are on duty?

A. It is not possible to visit all these places every day, but I try to visit some.

Q. Of course, the point is too that if, for example, you are moving from the Melting Pot Foundation in Atlantic Road to the Methodist Church in Railton Road, you are walking?

A. Yes.

Q. Always walking?

A. Yes.

Q. So that you get the chance, as you walk from place to place, to say "Hello" or stop for a chat with people whom you meet along the way?

A. Yes.

Q. Really that is the essence of home beat success, is it not: it is meeting people now and then, a bit of a chat and a bit of "Hello", that sort of thing?

A. That is the way I see it.

Q. Over 10 years you must have really got to know quite a lot of people who frequent that part of Brixton?

A. Yes, I do.

Q. You also issue parking tickets. Is that right?

A. Yes.

Q. What happens is this after a while. You get to know people. If there is a bit of bother you can probably step in and have a quiet word and sometimes you can sort out a bit of trouble without any need to arrest, if it is minor?

A. That is true.

Q. You do not take the view that everyone should be arrested at every single possible opportunity?

A. I take the view that that last thing I do is to take out a pocket book and report someone.

Q. Because you prefer to try and prevent breaches of the law, and your method is by doing it through friendship, acquaintanceship, chats and that sort of thing?

A. Yes.

Q. Getting on with people?

A. Yes.

Q. In fact you take the view that if you get on with people it is more likely to put you in a position to try and help people to stop incidents, is it not?

A   Yes.

Q. Then you have got lots of friends in the area that you can go to if you need a bit of help?

A. Yes.

Q. So by and large you prefer not to take your pocket book out. If it becomes necessary, obviously you have to?

A. Yes, that is true.

Q. But you would do your utmost throughout to try and avoid an incident of breaches of the law if you could?

A. Yes.

Q. By friendly persuasion?

A. Yes.

Q. I think it is right that in those 10 years that you have been walking that area – and you know it is supposed to be called the Front Line – environmentally, housing-wise, it is a pretty horrific area, is it not?

A. Yes, it is.

Q. The 10 years of walking and visiting in the Front Line area has not all been day-time, has it? Some of it has been evening?

A. That is right, and for the last six or seven years I have been taking part in late-night raids on the clubs down there as well.

Q. But on the normal home beat situation you have been walking during the evenings too?

A. Yes.

Q. And as you say, you have taken part in raids?

A. Yes, many raids.

Q. Having that kind of acquaintanceship with the community, both friendly persuasion and raids, you yourself have never been attacked in those 10 years by a single person, have you?

A. No.

Q. You have never been assaulted once in 10 years?

A. In that particular area, no. I was once attacked in Shakespeare Road, but that was six years ago.

Q. Would that be the only one in 10 years?

A. Yes.

Q. So that if you multiplied 10 years by the number of times you have walked up and down and the number of people you have met, really it has been a good, friendly time?

A. A very friendly time.

Q. You may have been called silly names on occasions, but I suppose you have not bothered too much with that?

A. No.

Q. You no doubt take the view that if you are called "white trash" or something silly like that, you must react violently to any silly abuse?

A. I got called much worse in Australia.

Q. That is where the Special Patrol Group should be sent – down under! You have been on the beat for ten years. In those 10 years 60% of your beat is black, or Afro-Asian.

A. Migrants from many countries – Italian, Greek, French, German.

Q. It is really a cosmopolitan area.

A. Yes.

Q. The reason that you have got on so well for ten years is partly because of your casual, friendly personality. I am sure that you will accept that. The second reason, however, is that people, regardless of race or colour, if approached in a friendly manner, they are reasonably friendly in return, by and large.

A. 90% are. You are still going to get a few who are not friendly.

Q. Generally, bearing in mind the number of years and the facts of nationality, race and colour, you have a friendly response?

A. Yes.

Q. From West Indians, Asians, the lot?

A. Yes.

Q. Young and old?

A. Yes.

Q. You said that you have never been assaulted or attacked apart from six years ago in Shakespeare Road. Your priority, therefore, is to keep the peace.

A. Yes.

Q. You are a peace officer?

A. Yes.

Q. You would not deliberately, and you obviously have not in those ten years, taken any steps to excite people. You would not want that to happen.

A. I would not think so.

Q. Because you would not wish to bring trouble on your patch unnecessarily?

A. No.

Q. Everybody is better off if the police and the community are on friendly terms.

A. Yes.

Q. For example, you would not stop 2,000 people, if you could physically, in five days without rhyme or reason, would you?

A. I do not know what the circumstances were.

LORD SCARMAN: I do not think it is suggested that any one officer stopped 2,000 people. Mr. Narayan, you have made your point extremely well. It is a pity to put a debating point like that to a police constable.

MR. NARAYAN: It may be that Mr. Brown is the best person to consult about Railton Road from the police side, I would suggest. What I am putting to you is this. As you went along on your ten years in the Railton Road area you would only go up to some one if you saw them breaking the law. Then you would have to, would you not?

A. Yes.

Q. And if you saw them behaving suspiciously?

A. Yes.

Q. That is your duty?

A. Yes.

Q. What you would never do is simply pick on someone and search him – out of the blue?

A. I think that you are referring to Operation Swamp '81. I would say that the officers employed on that were doing a particular job. They were working in areas with a very high crime rate. The only way to get results is by stopping people.

Q. I did not ask you for a view of the officers on Swamp '81. They can answer for themselves when they are sitting where you are sitting in due course. What I am asking you is this. You, anxious to keep the peace, would never deliberately excite people. Take those Rastas playing football. Once you went up to them and they unpacked the crates you did not go and search the lot of them or any of them, did you?

A. No.

Q. You would not simply search someone out of the blue unless you had a reason?

A. That is right.

Q. Because if you wanted to disturb the peace of your patch, if you wanted to start a riot, one of the best ways of starting a riot would be to stop 2,000 innocent citizens very fast. You would then have a riot on your hands, would you not?

A. So it seems from what happened.

Q. Knowing that is your patch you would not go around with iron bars in plastic carrier bags as you go up and down your duty? You would not show the public that you had iron bars on you, would you?

A. I have never done that.

Q. That would be calculated to excite people. Is that right?

A. If it happened it would.

LORD SCARMAN: If a police officer went around with an iron bar in a plastic bag you would consider that to be misconduct of a very, very serious kind?

A. I would, my lord.

MR. NARAYAN: In fact you would have to arrest that officer for carrying an offensive weapon. If you saw a peaceful crowd, including women and children, milling about and not obstructing the traffic – milling about peacefully – you would not charge into that crowd with truncheons, would you?

A. No.

Q. That could start a riot?

A. It could cause trouble.

Q. The men in the crowd would protect their women and children. That is right, is it not?

A. Yes.

Q. You did say that the training system of taking young officers on the home beat scene stopped five or six years ago. Is that right?

A. I think so, yes.

Q. Did that correspond with the coming of Commander Adams to Lambeth?

A. No, it was before that time. It was because of the shortage of manpower.

Q. As far as Thursday was concerned, apparently the Rastas situation was peacefully resolved.

A. Yes.

Q. With no incident?

A. No.

Q. I suppose if you had gone charging about there could have been an incident but you played it cool.

A. There were forty of them and two of us. It was better to play it cool.

Q. But could you have summoned reinforcements if you had wanted to.

A. There was no need.

Q. You played it cool and it was peacefully resolved within the law. Lawfully resolved, peacefully resolved.

Q. Can we come now to Friday, please. You said that you came on duty at 12 noon. I am trying to add up your times because they do not make sense to me at the moment. You came on duty at 12 o'clock and you walked the beat for how long?

A. For three and a half hours approximately.

Q. That would bring you to 3.30.

A. But I did not leave the station immediately. I had some correspondence and other things to deal with.

Q. You would have gone out later in the afternoon?

A. Yes.

Q. You were called to Railton Road because you heard that there had been some kind of trouble with a stabbing.

A. I was not called personally but I heard the messages coming over about trouble in Railton Road so I made my way there.

Q. If you as the home beat officer were there you might know some of the people and cool it.

A. Yes.

Q. That would be your intention. Aften ten years you would not like unnecessary trouble on your patch.

A. That is right.

Q. When you got there the stabbed youth had been taken away. Is that right?

A. Yes.

Q. Did you learn that he had been taken to hospital?

A. Later on. It was all a bit confused when I first arrived.

Q. When you first arrived did you hear the allegation that the police were not interested in taking him to hospital?

A. No.

Q. You did not hear that?

A. No. I heard that the next day.

Q. From people there?

A. Yes.

Q. People who talked to you quite willingly?

A. Yes.

Q. And peacefully?

A. Yes.

Q. That is the situation and when you get there it is all over.

A. Yes.

Q. You went back to the station from Railton Road. Is that right?

A. Yes.

Q. When you left Railton Road was it peaceful?

A. Yes. There was no trouble there when I left.

Q. You must have seen some of the people that you knew.

A. No. There were lots of shops there. Do you know the shops?

A. Yes.

Q. Did you make one or two enquiries to make sure that things were peaceful?

A. I went straight back to Brixton Police Station.

Q. You, as home beat officer, would not leave your beloved, peaceful patch unless it was safe to do so.

A. It appeared peaceful at that time.

Q. You went back to the station and then were asked to accompany some officers from M Division.

A. Yes.

Q. To where were you guiding them?

A. I can remember that there were about six Transit vehicles and I was on the first one. We were given a particular area to patrol.

A. Was this part of Swamp?

A. No.

Q. These were M Division?

A. It was the serial that I was attached to.

Q. But you are L Division?

A. Yes.

Q. Is M Division Wandsworth?

A. No. M Division is Peckham.

Q. Have you been asked to accompany officers in this way from different Divisions in a vehicle before?

A. Yes.

Q. Was it a night after night thing?

A. No. This was a one-off situation.

Q. When was the last time you were asked to do that before?

A. I would say about three years ago. There was a demonstration in the Brixton area and they wanted people who knew the area.

Q. One can see the reason for that – a demonstration. The last time you had been asked to do it was three years before. Is that right?

A. Yes.

Q. This, in the context of a three year gap, was something new for you. Is that right?

A. Yes.

Q. Driving round as you did you came across this demonstration outside the Ritz Cinema and you radioed in to Inspector Scotchford about a trade dispute demonstration?

A. Yes.

Q. That is exactly what it was – a trade dispute demonstration.

A. As it turned out I think that it was.

Q. You did not arrest anyone?

A. No.

Q. Was it perfectly lawful?

A. Yes.

Q. In fact it was citizens exercising their right of protest.

A. Yes.

Q. Is that the way that you saw it?

A. Apart from one person who, for some reason unbeknown to me, became abusive.

Q. That was the man who you had known for five years before.

A. Yes.

Q. Is he based locally?

A. Yes. He lives in Shakespeare Road.

Q. Even though you were abused and could lawfully have arrested someone you did not?

A. No.

Q. You ignored that?

A. Yes.

Q. Despite the fact that it was peaceful and lawful Inspector Scotchford on the radio asked you to obtain the details and the names of organisers of that demonstration?

A. This is quite normal.

Q. Even a peaceful and lawful demo – you have got to get names?

A. We tried to get them and they are recorded.

Q. Why? If they are not breaking the law why did you do this?

A. I do not know why. It is one of the rules of the Metropolitan Police.

Q. Is it intelligence gathering?

A. No. It is not that.

Q. If it is peaceful and lawful you still do this?

A. Yes. I think the reason is to find out what their intentions are. Sometimes they have marches afterwards.

Q. Can we now leave Friday and turn to Saturday morning at 6.30.

A. Yes.

Q. Mr. Brown, I have been asking you questions on the basis of your ten years as a home beat officer in this area. By the time you reported for duty at 6.30 on Saturday morning you knew of the incident on the Friday night?

A. I did.

Q. Did you know by the time that you came back on duty on Saturday morning that the youth had ended up in hospital?

A. Yes.

Q. That he was taken there by his friends?

A. Yes.

Q. Not by the police?

A. No.

Q. So far as you were concerned that incident was over?

A. Yes.

Q. Nobody had been arrested?

A. No.

Q. And the youth was in hospital?

A. Yes.

Q. Did you go straight out on to your beat at 6.30 or did you stay in the station for a while?

A. Within about ten minutes.

Q. You went out going on for 7 o'clock. That Saturday morning the weather was beautiful, was it not?

A. Beautiful.

Q. You are walking your beat including Railton Road. Is that right?

A. Yes.

Q. With P/Con. Thorning?

A. Yes.

Q. Did you spend the whole day on that beat?

A. I did, yes.

Q. You know that Saturday morning and afternoon in Brixton, especially in the market area and the Railton Road area, is choc-a-bloc with people coming in to shop?

A. Yes.

Q. Virtually that market area on a lovely Saturday morning is crammed full of shoppers. That is right, is it not?

A. Yes.

Q. Despite that there were no incidents at all?

A. None that I heard of.

Q. Everybody was going about their normal business.

A. Yes.

Q. Everything was as peaceful as can be?

A. Yes.

Q. Glorious weather?

A. Yes.

Q. Happy Brixton?

A. Yes.

Q. As pretty as a picture, the way you like it?

A. Yes.

Q. No trouble at all. Not a sign, a whisper or a smell?

A. No.

Q. Really lovely on that Saturday morning?

A. Yes.

Q. You would know because you like your patch to be lovely and you would know if something was up and you would try and squash it if you could?

A. Yes.

Q. Unfortunately there were a large number of police officers in and around the crowds on that Saturday morning?

A. There were.

Q. Were they in uniform or plain clothes or both?

A. I saw only uniformed officers.

Q. Quite a lot?

A. Quite a lot.

Q. There was no crime or crimes or any breaches of law being committed that you could see or hear of?

A. I did not see anything.

Q. Was there a swamping of that area with police officers on Saturday morning?

A. There were more police officers than normal. However, I would not say an excessive amount.

Q. A larger number than normal?

A. Yes.

Q. I think that 112 extra officers came on the streets at 2 o'clock on that Saturday. Did you know that?

A. I did not know that.

Q. Here we are, market day, people, crowds, no incidents. You must have been pretty pleased with life because this is your patch and you have a nice peaceful day?

A. Yes.

Q. The last thing that you would have done, or wanted to see done, is break that peace up?

A. Yes.

Q. Brixton on a Saturday morning, when everything is going well, is a beautiful place.

LORD SCARMAN: We have had that about six times. I am not a

jury. I am a judge and when I hear the thing once it is enough.

MR. NARAYAN: My Lord, yes. I am afraid I am infatuated with Brixton on a Saturday morning. When you left your beat was it at 3 o'clock?

A. Yes, about that time.

Q. So had you spent about nine hours, excepting for meal breaks, on the beat?

A. It was about 8¼ hours, I left just before.

Q. Really the whole of your time?

A. Yes.

Q. Nothing wrong at all?

A. No.

Q. May I just come to this. You go off duty and you go home?

A. Yes.

Q. As Mr. Blom-Cooper ascertained from you, I think, you have a telephone at home?

A. Yes.

Q. You could be called in easily. You have a car you could drive in, could you?

A. That is right, yes.

Q. If you had been called to trouble on your own patch, you would have willingly responded?

A. Yes, I would have.

Q. Because you have that one advantage over all other police officers in that that is your patch and you know the people there.

A. I know a lot of people.

Q. You would confidently say that if you were called in to trouble in Railton Road, you would feel able to at least approach people with a view to talking?

A. The people I knew, I probably would have done, yes.

Q. Including the shop keepers and all that?

A. Yes.

Q. You would be willing always to try and approach people on your beat to resolve matters amicably?

A. Yes.

Q. Your willingness must be known to your superior officers, surely?

A. I believe so, yes.

Q. But not a tinkle on the Saturday, nor on the Sunday?

A. No.

Q. This break in duty from 3 pm on the Saturday to the Tuesday morning, had it been a planned weekend leave?

A. Yes.

Q. Planned by you for weeks?

A. No, it was just a normal weekend leave that occurs every now and again.

Q. You were not deliberately put out of the way to let the troops move in?

A. No, definitely not.

MR. NARAYAN: Thank you.

Part IV

The Bar's Monopoly

Part IV

The Bar's Monopoly

I have dealt elsewhere with the incompetence that attends certain
members of the Bar and there is now growing public debate as to
whether the Bar's Monopoly of advocacy in Crown and High Court
should not be broken in the public interest but without sacrificing
high standards. The "high standards" of advocacy argument is the
Bar's response to the "break the monopoly" thrust of the Law
Society's attack and all that is worth examining really is the integrity
of the Bar's response.

Who are barristers and what are they? What is their educational
background? Is it different from the Law Society's? If not, why not?
If not, then are solicitor and barrister really two different animals or
can they easily interchange roles? If they can easily interchange roles,
then what is the public interest argument for retraining one profession
for the price of two?

Barristers and solicitors now begin life with a degree in law obtained
after a three-year course at university or polytechnic; the law they
study is the same and they are marked by the same tutuors at the same
time in the same way. There is therefore absolutely no difference
whatsoever during their degree course.

After this three-year stint, the would-be barrister then does a year at
law school at the Inns of Court but there is no significant difference in
the subjects they study there and the subjects the solicitors take at
their Law Society Finals examination except for conveyancing and
book-keeping! These two subjects, needless to say, can be swotted up
in less than three months by those barristers who wish to change-over
and they often are. Apart from this, there is training in Court
Procedure and some advocacy for the would-be Barrister. The
solicitor, incidentally, spends an additional two years studying after

university but the barrister only one so that, if length of qualifying study is anything to go by, then the solicitor wins hands down every time.

What is this special magic that barristers have that equips them and them alone for the robe and wig? If they have no extra special training, what marks them out for preferment as exclusive enjoyers of the total monopoly of advocacy in Crown and High Court? Are they more honest than solicitors? Clearly , not even the Bar would seek to lean on this presumption! Are they more able? I leave this open for public debate.

The answer is that the barrister's preserve has been traditionally a monopoly of the sons and daughters of the privileged but less so today. The pretence is kept up that the Holy Grail of wig and gown is the best costume to fit one for the Judiciary and thus are solicitors largely denied the right to judgeships at the end of their careers.

What is the service the Bar performs for the public?

The only service is one of advocacy and more time to research law. Why should a solicitor who is absolutely dazzling at criminal law be deprived of the opportunity to represent his client before judge and jury? And why should the public pay twice for both solicitor and barrister?

And why should an extremely able barrister not himself be able to begin work on the criminal trial without the intervention of a solicitor? And, again the question, why should the public pay twice over for the same service? If the solicitor must at some stage drop out of active work on a case, why should he continue to receive payment for simply dancing attendance on counsel in court? And, three times over, why should the public pay twice-over for the same, single service?

The answer is that solicitors and barristers can switch roles at the drop of a wig if they wish and they should be allowed to do so, if only in the public interest and for saving of the public purse.

I would argue that the American "Attorney" system, without the artificial intermediary of "solicitors" is the most economic, efficient and accountable, makes for more competition and offers the public higher standards.

Part V

Trial Classique, Birmingham Crown Court,
November 1984

PART V
Trial Classique

The Trial of Lionel Brown

On the 13th November, 1984, two men, George Tomkins, a Geordie, and Lionel Webb, a Barbadian, walked free of charges of conspiracy to rob and kindred offences at Birmingham Crown Court in a trial that lasted five weeks. Mr Justice Skinner, perhaps the most eminent personification of judicial fairness and graciousness, presided. There was a jury of eight whites, four black, including one Asian.

The trial is a classic of its kind in that it had everything worthy of study and emulation by the aspiring barrister for the defence and that is why I take the trouble of setting it out in a separate section.

Let me make is clear that I neither associate nor disassociate this book with what was said on both sides during this trial – I merely recite the narrative as given in public and as reprinted by the newspapers – all except the "enlightened and liberal" *Observer* which paid no attention to the heavy allegations canvassed in the trial but chose in its "enlightened" wisdom to do a story instead on defence lawyers drinking with the jury after the jury were discharged – a practice which lawyers (and police and press too!) have indulged in right across the country in very many cases. Sometimes the acquittal of blacks on serious charges raises hackles in the most "enlightened" and "liberal" quarters and, although it is not for me to say, it may be that blacks and black organisations in Britain and internationally should carefully review the question of support for so-called "liberal" newspapers which represent themselves as friendly to blacks and other minorities.

However, *Observer* or no *Observer*, let the truth be told! The story of the trial began, as was set out at court, with telephone calls to the Serious Crimes Squad of the West Midlands Police from a known criminal whom I shall call Joseph Smith. Smith was on the run from police who wanted him for an assortment of minor offences including credit card and cheque offences, and an alleged assault on a young detective in Coventry, and his family had been pulled in by police. He rang the police to offer to do "a deal" in that he stated (and this was all tape recorded by the police and transcripts made available at court) that if the police would allow him out of his own charges he (Smith) would lead them to an alleged armed robber, one Lionel Webb and Webb's alleged partners-in-crime. To be fair, the police officers who taped the calls with this informer told the Crown Court that he was only leading him on and that he (the officer) had not the slightest intention of assisting the informer to have charges dropped against him. However, a detailed and searching examination was carried out of the transcripts of the conversations and the defence set great store by their contention that there had in fact been a "deal" between police and informer.

However, part of the arrangement between the officer and Smith included the arrangement that police would wait and watch outside an address in Small Heath from eight-thirty one morning and would then follow the informer and criminals to the scene of an alleged robbery where police would swoop on the unsuspecting villains. But, according to the prosecution case, the informer was merely "pretending" to conspire and really, known to police, was not himself guilty enough to be arrested himself on the spot because of his arranged pretence! And thereby hangs a tale because the astute reader will follow immediately that for there to be a conspiracy there has to be more than one! (And so the fairminded Mr Justice Skinner directed the jury.)

The problem with police denial of a "deal" however, was, as advanced at trial, that police, although meeting with their informer outside Weoley Castle Post Office, declined to arrest him and he walked free of arrest and vanished into the London Metropolitan area!

As I say, the astute law student will sit up and note that, with the police informer not being "in" on the alleged conspiracy before armed police swooped on Webb hiding in the back of an old transit van outside the Post Office, then the prosecution have to find a second conspirator, even if an unknown one. But the prosecution contended that there was such a second conspirator in the form of one Wesley Augustus Black, a known friend and associate of the defendant Webb. The trouble was that Black could not be found. But, nevertheless the prosecution ventured the evidence that Black was in on the conspiracy since a police log showed that police had followed Black and had seen his blue Capri roaring off from the scene of the alleged intended crime. The problem was, asserted the defence, that the police observation log was clearly faked and the defence submitted that the jury could not rely on this log to found a finding of the existence of a second conspirator. So, with one of their large guns well and truly spiked the prosecution case lumbered on.

The prosecution intoned, in the darkest sepulchral tones of that distinguished prosecutor Mr Igor Judge QC, ably assisted by the almost equally distinguished Mr Peter Crane, that the defendant Webb was caught "redhanded" in the back of the van disguised up to his eyeballs and in possession of a loaded shotgun. The problem was, said the defence, that Webb was arrested simply sitting in the back of the van near to the alleged location of the shotgun find and, although the money-carrying Post Office van, the alleged prospective victim of the conspiracy, had arrived, delivered its money and gone away (according to defence evidence), Webb had not made a single move to get out of the van and rob his alleged intended victims. Webb told the jury that he saw some "white men in cars" driving and then realised he had been "set-up" by the informer and had simply refused to move a stolen van "with a prize in the offing" later but that he had had no idea of the alleged intended robbery of the Post Office van.

But, muttered the prosecution's beaten men feebly as they clutched at straws, Webb had confessed to police in what the defence called "manufactured verbals" – indeed, the prosecution proudly declaimed, not only had Webb confessed to the Post Office van conspiracy but he had confessed to a few other robberies as well! As Webb's defence barrister put it (and I am not allowed to tell you his name!) "my client has allegedly freely confessed not only to these robberies but to the sinking of the *Titanic* and the wreck of the *Marie Celeste* as well!"

The police had alleged that Webb had confessed "verbally" in four successive interviews but that he would not sign notes of his alleged confessions. Webb said that he had simply given his name as John Smith but, apart from a few choice obscenities, had not confessed to anything. He claimed that the officers had promised him to "manufacture such beautiful verbals that they hoped he (Webb) would congratulate them on it at court!" Webb claimed that one police officer had promised to "verbal him up" and that "there is nothing you can do about it – I am a police officer." The officer denied all of Webb's allegations.

Even so, chimed the last bell of the prosecution's wilting clock,

Webb had been identified on identification parade by a security guard. But, responded the defence, that same security guard could not be relied on because he had claimed before the magistrates court that he had been shown photographs of black men before the parade while at the trial he retracted this. Further, Webb's co-defendant claimed that the security guard had identified the "police informer" as one of the men and then apparently changed his mind.

The jury retired overnight and returned verdicts of "Not Guilty" on all the seven charges against both men while armed police ringed the dock of Birmingham Crown Court. The two men literally walked free through a gangplank of about thirty police officers who formed a most intimidating presence as the jury returned with their verdicts. This victory is in its way a high tribute to the industry and expertise of Webb Defence Solicitor, Ajmal Mian, who is rapidly earning the reputation of being one of Birmingham's most trusted defence solicitors, not to mention the tenacity and attack of Defence Counsel Michael Wolkind who, with his charismatic junior, Jeremy Ornstein, fought a brilliant pitched battle for Tomkins' acquittal. Steve Daley, one of Birmingham's fastest-rising solicitor stars, instructed and Barrister Mike Magloire was assiduous junior to Lionel Webb's devastating Defence Barrister, he who must not be named!

The local reporters who were awaiting convictions and long prison sentences were visibly distraught that an aggressive (and arguably brilliant) defence had robbed them of their journalistic prey so they went hunting for "an angle" on the acquittals. They had sat in court and witnessed the most grave defence allegations against police misconduct but they, the Guardians of Truth, chose to ignore all the defence allegations. If these be the Guardians of the Lamp of Freedom then one should move one's Citizen Lamp to a safer place.

This case raised the most important questions concerning police use of informers to "set-up" robberies, issues concerning "verbal admissions", issues concerning identification evidence and yet the press stayed silent. This book of record notes that the acquittal of blacks on serious charges in the courts of England is never attended by a fair press – they , like vultures, seek only black corpses and they are the very carrion–crows of what should be an honourable profession; not all the press are like that but too many Crime Reporters are of this vintage. Britain's minorities are entitled to stop buying newspapers who adopt this one-sided stance – it is a fact of life that the only newspaper which carry the acquittals of blacks in such sensational cases are campaigning newspapers like the *Caribbean Times*. If the *Caribbean Times* can carry such an important story why cannot the

Observer or the *Birmingham Post*? I leave it to the public to demand the answers and, if none be forthcoming, to stop buying newspapers which will not tell The Whole Truth. Both the *Observer* and the *Birmingham Post* are, of course, admirable papers in their own way but this significant defect must be corrected.

P.S. The police informer, Joseph Smith, was himself sentenced to a total of five years' imprisonment.

Part VI

The Epilogue
The Last Word

The Last Word

The Epilogue

Having dealt now with the strictly academic side of the qualities of the Advocate it needs now only finally to deal with the political, socio-cultural and economic radar's nest within which the Advocate addresses the members of the jury. Unless one has a keen and swift perception of these matters which now follow one cannot aspire to the heights of advocacy to which this book is dedicated.

On the 10th September, 1984, Mr Peter Ackroyd of London, SW1, wrote to *The Times* of London:

"Your report of the strongly-worded advice to police officers not to be Freemasons . . . prompts the question as to whether the same advice should not be given to judges, barristers and other members of the legal profession . . . the secrecy involved in Masonic activities must always provoke doubt about their propriety."

The day before, September 9th, investigative journalists David Leigh and Paul Lashmar had written in *The Observer*

"Many DPP officials are Masons . . . complaints about Freemasons to Scotland Yard have centred on hints of . . . corrupt relationships with criminals in masonic lodges . . . the former DPP was a prominent Freemason . . . the present deputy DPP and one of the key assistant Directors are both said to be masons . . . Sir Ian Percival QC, MP, (a former Solicitor General) and Lord Whitelaw are masons . . . dozens of magistrates, judges and prosecuting solicitors are rank and file masons and we have identified at least 36 judges who have held senior masonic offices . . . they range from the House of Lords (Lord Templeman) to the Old Bailey (Judge Abdela) and the High Court (the former Lord Chief Justice, Lord Widgery)".

The reader will have noticed that Defence Barristers are NOT listed as part of the Freemasons, neither, incidentally, are black, working-class or women lawyers – in fact, the pattern of membership follows precisely the hierarchy of those afforded promotion within the legal profession although it is not for me to say whether or not this is mere coincidence for, as Shakespeare's Mark Anthony said: "they are all honourable men."

Of course, some people outside the profession are heard to say the Bar does not need formal membership of Freemasonry because "it is its own Freemasonry and the Judges the High Officers of that Order." It is often said among non-lawyers that "the Bar is the most elitist, exclusive and incestuous profession in England". Whether these be informed or responsible comments on this "honourable" profession is not for me to say but it can be contended that if the appointment of British judges by secret men reading secret reports in secret places is anything to go by then the first ritual of Freemasonry is made out by the way in which the Lord Chancellor's Office appoints certain lawyers to Judgeships while others are ignored.

If there is a case for investigating Freemasonry in the police then it is for the public to judge whether Mr Peter Ackroyd's comments in *The Times* are so far right or wrong.

If one investigates the different ranks within the British legal profession then it is true that one discovers a substantial element of Freemasonry membership – whether this is good, bad or undesirable is not for me to say; indeed, it can probably be argued that the Bed of Freemasonry is the Very Rock on which to build a Judiciary of honour, integrity and high intellectual endeavour.

From information supplied by my Freemason contacts, of 80-odd High Court Judges, some 30 are said to be Freemasons, of 326 Circuit Judges some 75 are said to be Freemasons, of some 456 Recorders in the Crown Courts some 137 are said to be Freemasons, of over 70 Stipendiary Magistrates at least 12 are said to be Freemasons, of about 600 Queen's Counsel over 100 are said to be Freemasons and the reputed membership extends in similar strength throughout the ranks of Treasury Counsel, Clerks to the Justices, officers of the D.P.P. and, of course, police officers. Defence barristers are NOT listed within their ranks!

In amplification of the above, one can seek statistical support from Stephen Knight's controversial bestseller *The Brotherhood* (Panther – Granada Publishing) and see what he says first about Freemasonry in the Lord Chancellor's Department (Page 176); "When barristers join the right Bar Lodge he can be certain of getting on first name terms with scores of influential judges and with large numbers of my colleagues in the Lord Chancellor's Department . . . this is a right and proper method for men of integrity to come to the Bench". Knight's masonic contact goes on: "Where better to find out if a man has these qualities than in Lodge?"

Concerning the police, Knight writes (quoting an informant on Birmingham City Police): "You cannot possibly rise in the CID unless you are in a Lodge." He quotes Police Superintendent David Webb, the well-known champion of community policing in Handsworth: "In the City of Birmingham there are hundreds of policemen who are members of Freemasonry."

Of course, the complication with Freemasonry is that if judges and policemen Freemasons of the same Lodge get together, as they might, under the mantle of Brotherhood, who knows quite what is said by whom about what – secret rituals and secrets kept under an oath which reads: "I further solemnly swear that I will not write those secrets (of Freemasonry) . . . under no less a penalty, on the violation of them . . . than that of having my throat cut across, my tongue torn out by the root, and buried in the sand of the sea at low water mark."

"Masonry so permeates so many revered British institutions from the Crown downwards that a grave masonic scandal could in modern circumstances involve popular revulsion against the whole established order, Government and business. Second, the proportion of Masons to non-Masons in some professions and other walks of life including areas of Government, appears to have reached a critical point: the point at which people believe themselves obliged to join Freemasonry, no longer voluntarily, but from a feeling of compulsion." One cannot be sure about quite how many judges are Freemasons or how many police officers, if any, they meet with in Lodges and one cannot know how many Barristers and Solicitors are either but, if Knight's book is anything to go by, then the general public might well feel that the legal profession and the police should keep an Open Book on Freemasonry membership.

I would submit that membership of Freemasonry must surely run contrary to the need for a Lord Chief Justice (Widgery) or a Law Lord (Templeman) or an Old Bailey Judge (Abdela) or a Law Officer (Percival) or D.P.P. (Skelhorn) to be "above it all" and to be seen to be so. And it cannot be right for Barristers and Solicitors either since this makes mockery of the Bar's strictures against Barristers consorting with Solicitors (with its implications of touting for business.)

While Judges *in public* sit above it all, while Barristers and Solicitors keep their distance *in public*, while Judges sit *in public* aloof from Police Constables, Freemasonry can make this a mockery and a shabby pretence since a cat (a Police Constable) may now, at least in theory, not just look, but embrace, a King (or a Law Lord!).

It's not just the potential fraternisation between Freemason Judges with Freemason police officers that might offend but it is the shroud of secrecy that surrounds it. I would argue that justice by Judges cannot be seen to be done if they are parties to such secret societies.

Secrecy is the enemy of democracy and the friend of impropriety, and Judges in particular should, at the minimum, publicly declare the fact of their membership of Masonry and whether police officers are members of their respective Lodges. Only in this way can public anxiety, like that of Mr. Peter Ackroyd, be answered.

If enquiries or declarations were to reveal that sitting Judges and serving Police Officers (always potential witnesses at Crown Courts) shared the same Lodges or met at masonic meetings or functions then the public might feel that such Judges should be alert to guard jealously that high detachment and objectivity which is the hallmark of the English judiciary.

It would be interesting to know whether any Old Bailey Judges have ever met police officers at their Lodges (not that anything improper is being suggested), whether the D.P.P. staff responsible for the non-prosecution of Brixton Police Officers (who smashed up Frontline homes and property) meet with Police Officers at their Lodges, whether Lord Whitelaw does (or did, when he was Home Secretary), and whether the former Chief Justice (Widgery) shared membership with Police Officers.

Masonic Lodges cannot be dismissed as being mere "clubs", on a par with "Garrick's" or the "R.A.C." – Lodges are a "brotherhood" so close, so tight and so secret that they might create and sustain a most unhealthy effect on the ability to be detached and objective towards others outside the world of the Lodge.

This is not to decry or denigrate the very honourable work Freemasons do for charity nor to suggest that Freemasons is improper or dishonourable in any way; nor indeed that judicial membership is by itself improper. It may also well be that Freemasonry cultivates the very qualities of probity, integrity and industry that society needs, and it is conceded that people of the highest repute, including the Royal Family, are members.

But, despite everything, Oaths of Loyalty to members of secret societies could involve emotional conflict if not professional difficulties and it is submitted that Judges, paid and promoted for carefully cultivated detachment and objectivity, should not be members or, if they are, they should openly declare it.

But it must be said, although some police officers and some prosecuting Barristers receive perceptively more cordial treatment from certain Old Bailey judges, it is not known whether this is the product of Freemasonry or simply old acquaintances being naturally and unobjectively chummy with each other.

And when one speaks of the British Judiciary one must have in mind certain recent controversial instances of high public interest.

It was said in Brixton pubs, for example, that former Judge Bruce Campbell QC, he of the whisky and cigarettes and unpaid VAT duty, should have been imprisoned immediately as opposed to being awarded a half-pension by the Lord Chancellor's Office. Whether he should or not is open to public debate – I can only say that the ordinary folk say that they are entitled to hope that their "betters" will be imprisoned with as much swiftness and firmness as they would be if caught in the same boat (or yacht!).

Much comment was also made in pubs and market-places at the way in which Mr Justice Croome-Johnson summed up in the case of the police officers who were acquitted of offences against Mr Stephen Waldorf and it was even argued that the judge had shown pro-police bias. Similar comments flew around in political circles when Mr Justice Cantley was said to have almost directed the acquittal of former Liberal Leader Jeremy Thorpe on the most serious charges. For myself, I find nothing to criticise.

Of course, the most controversial Judicial utterances of late came from arguably one of the greatest British Judges of this century, Lord Denning (not so much a Mason, more a brickdropper!), when he castigated black jurors serving on the Bristol Riots trial. Denning's utterances were openly attacked as racist by the Society of Black Lawyers' then Chairman, barrister Sibghat Kadri, and Kadri's courageous attack may well have led to Denning's premature resignation from the distinguished office which he himself had graced with much nobility and distinction. I personally would prefer to describe Denning's remarks as the product of a mind gracious and brilliant in many areas but ignorant of this particular episode; and the incident is well worth examining in some detail.

The Trial of the Bristol 12 took place before Mr Justice Stocker, an eminently fairminded judge, in the Bristol Crown Court. A number of defendants, black and white and one woman, were accused of rioting in the St Paul's area of Bristol. The trial attracted much interest.

Application had been made earlier to Judge Stocker for blacks to be included in the prospective panel of jurors and he had most courteously and helpfully granted the application in an extremely enlightened and liberal judgement.

When the day of Trial came, defence barristers utilised their statutory right of jury challenge to ensure the presence of at least four blacks on the twelve-man jury and so the trial began.

During the trial, heavy allegations were made against the police and the jury acquitted eight of the twelve defendants, disagreeing on the remaining four. (The D.P.P. later elected "not to proceed" again against the remaining four.)

Lord Denning clearly thought there had been a denial of Justice and he went on to attack the verdicts of acquittal in an untypically irresponsible way: ". . . the defence used their rights of challenge . . . to empanel *a number of black jurors* . . . this jury *so constituted* went on to acquit the real trouble-makers . . ." Astonishing words from a leading Judge trained to act (and speak!) only on the evidence (for Denning never once set foot in the court of trial and had no way of judging the quality of the evidence.) Further, Denning was never privy to what went on in the jury room and so could not honestly ascribe to jurors, black or white, their contributions to the acquittals. But where this legendary legal luminary went clearly judicially (and mathematically) wrong was to infer that the black jurors were to be pilloried for verdicts of acquittal also contributed to by eight white jurors! Denning's attack was clearly the product of judicial tittle-tattle and the open resentment of the prosecution lawyers that a quarter-of-a-million pounds of public money had not reaped a single conviction – his distinguished mind was clearly led astray by others. But the really alarming thing was that the entire Judiciary kept total silence and would not speak out against Denning's attack on black jurors.

Denning indeed had rationalised his attack by claiming that black jurors came from countries "where dishonesty was part of their way of life" and he had said expressly that blacks were not really suitable for jury service in the British courts. When myself and Sibghat Kadri looked for allies among MPs, judges and British lawyers, all was silence. The Bar Council of England, allegedly the trade union of all lawyers, refused to act. The Bristol Bar kept quiet. The Labour Party, the party of posturing hypocrisy, stayed mute. All was silence until the Society of Black Lawyers, led by Kadri, mounted its attack on ignorance and prejudice. And Fleet Street echoed the deafening silence.

But more was to come from the Denning stable since Lady Denning (an equally gracious and kind person) now entered into the race and gave an historic "judgement" on black lawyers. Her Ladyship, riding the same horse as his Lordship, gave the verdict that "black lawyers were not yet qualified for appointments to the Judiciary." And still all the Judiciary kept silent and Lord Hailsham's silence was the loudest silence of all.

I personally continue to have the highest personal regard for Lord Denning not only as one of the most distinguished judges of this century but also as a supreme source of charm and graciousness to the international student fraternity; knowing as I do how many Denning

Societies there are in Africa, Asia and the Caribbean and that he, above all, was the most wined and dined and honoured man by the Bars of the Third World, I regret his remarks as untypical and unthinking and even, perhaps, without malice; but a man of his advanced years can easily stumble into intellectual disorder.

It is not just his remarks on the Bristol jurors that causes unease but his calculated statement that "such people . . . come from countries where dishonesty is a way of life"! Since he was speaking of black jurors the countries he must have had in mind must have been Africa and Asia in particular, the very countries that had feted and honoured him.

What causes even more disquiet is that British political and legal circles must have condoned, if not endorsed, his remarks and this makes for permanent disquiet; and I do condemn the Judiciary and the parliamentarians who kept silent.

Lord Hailsham indeed, and no one has more regard for his genius and integrity than I, has denied his otherwise distinguished tenures of office by the general failure of his office so far to appoint blacks in significant numbers to the ranks of Queen's Counsel. This failure to appoint blacks is the very echo of Lady Denning's "judgement".

A member of the Bar (anxious not to be disbarred!) accuses an incumbent Lord Chancellor of racism at his peril, and I do NOT make this accusation against Lord Hailsham; yet I can quote the results of the Cobden Trust research report by Michael King and Colin May (as quoted by Peter Evans in *The Times* in March, 1985) which states that "there is evidence of racial discrimination in selecting and appointing magistrates." The report states that "some of the people appointed by the Lord Chancellor to do the selection are prejudiced against black people!" How very extraordinary; and one of course wonders whether this Legal AIDS is limited to those appointing magistrates or whether it could possibly extend to others responsible for judicial and other appointments. I only ask the question – I do not answer it! The next question is whether certain well-qualified black rejects might have been appointed if they had met their would-be "appointors" as brothers in the same Freemasonry Lodge – Freemasonry, after all, embraces all religions and could arguably be the antidote to the poison of racism. The answer, of course, is that if the Cobden Trust conclusions are correct, then it is a state of affairs that should not need membership of Freemasonry to put it right. On this question of black appointees, "God Bless America"! And an examination of the British courts on other aspects will reveal several other disturbing comparisons with the American courts across the water.

British Judges, as I have repeatedly pointed out, are appointed by secret process. While the Lord Chancellor's civil servants may well know the reasons for their preferment the public has no way of knowing and that defies democracy. American judges on the other hand are carefully scrutinised and elected – they "run" for office and are severely open to public scrutiny. Many a time even Presidential nominations to the American judiciary are opposed by hostile and alert Congress while the British House of Commons has no such power. One can only imagine what mincemeat socialist MP Dennis Skinner would make of certain new appointees.

The 27th February, 1985, saw President Reagan's appointee as U.S. Attorney General publicly grilled by an alert, astute and aggressive Congressional Committee before his appointment was confirmed . . . one ruefully longs for public grilling of similar British appointees! (No disrespect intended, Sir Michael!). But one fears that even the most left-wing MPs are terrified of taking on the British Judiciary and the British legal profession remains the Sacred Cow of the professions.

British courts will definitely not allow radio or television or cameras into the courtroom. When British television wants to film live courtroom scenes then they have to go to the United States, cameras, microphones and all. The reluctance of the British courts is glaringly contrasted with the openness of the Americans.

British lawyer MPs are obsessed with the restriction of the right of challenge of prospective jurors; even an "enlightened" Labour Government reduced the right of peremptory challenge from seven to three! Applications by minorities to be tried by their "peers" are met sometimes with cynicism or amusement in England while the Americans openly encourage the challenge of jurors on the basis of attitudes and prejudices. The British legal system skates over this question of prejudice, whether it be of race, class, sex or creed.

On the question of trial by jury no greater affront to the principles of democracy and the dignity of a people could be offended than by the setting-up of the Diplock courts in Northern Ireland and the abolition of the right to trial by jury for the people of Northern Ireland by the British "Masters". How can the same Government rationalise trial by jury in England and Wales and deny it to the Irish people? Is "trial by peers" a necessity for the English but a luxury to be denied to the colonised Irish? Taken jointly with the technical rape of Irish women internees (forcible intimate body searches) one has to look for comparison to the notorious Virginity Tests of Indian women at Heathrow Airport and the intimate body searches of blacks on the Brixton Frontline.

Anyone who doubts that Britain is an inherently racist society has only to look to British practices in Northern Ireland to realise that the British legal profession (now seeking under Lord Hailsham's leadership the abolition of jury trial in fraud cases), can campaign for trial by jury in any country save Northern Ireland. And both Labour and Tory parties have proved equally racist in their vicious approaches to the Irish people.

One other unfair aspect of the Criminal Trial in Northern Ireland is the continuing use of 'Supergrass' evidence against the freedom fighters of the I.R.A. – it does not take much imagination or high intelligence to know that the offer of high financial rewards (or forbearances to prosecute) might well induce any man to sell his soul to the devil (or Northern Ireland authorities) and lie his head off (and somebody else's life) away. Indeed, the prosecuting authorities on the mainland have to persuade British juries of other, supporting (corroborative) evidence, but their consciences and their logic vanish when dealing with the freedom struggle in Northern Ireland – supergrass evidence and the Diplock courts plus torture of Irish prisoners (see the European Court's judgement on British military detention and interrogation procedures) remain the two most illegal manifestations of Protestant racism against their fellow Christian (but Catholic) brothers.

The campaign to abolish trial by jury in fraud cases must be seen for what it is – the thin end of the wedge. While it is true that fraud cases attract a massive amount of paperwork and very lucid exposition by Counsel there remains as in all criminal trials the fundamental question of dishonesty which is best tried by a jury of twelve citizens. As both JUSTICE and the NCCL have said: "The question remains basically one of dishonesty and there is no evidence of a high acquittal rate in such trials. Indeed, the opposite is true in that there is a higher percentage of acquittals in crimes of violence cases than in fraud." Further the moment one allows the judges to be judges of the facts then those convicted might well allege judicial bias. No such allegation is possible against twelve fellow citizens.

The other danger is that judges will tend to be ruthless in their approach towards speeding up such trials, perhaps the real reason behind Lord Hailsham's proposals, and where speed of trial becomes a driving motivation then careful consideration of the minor intricacies of facts may well be unintentionally sacrificed. The fundamental objection I make to the abolition of the right of trial by jury is that it runs hard against the golden principle of trial of citizen by citizen . . . judges are not "peers" of the citizen and must never be exposed to allegations, well-founded or not, that a jury might have acquitted.

One can imagine the response that might have followed Clive Ponting's (hypothethetical) conviction at the hands of Mr. Justice McCowan – such a conviction might well have been greeted as a "policy decision" and could have led to the subsequent arrest and prosecution of MI5's Cathy Massiter for revealing secrets of phone-tapping and Special Branch files. In this sense, it can be said that the public (as jurors) make and unmake the law since, after Ponting's acquittal, Section 2 of the Official Secrets Act is now itself for the high-jump! It is in fact the Ponting verdict which dissuaded the Attorney General from a possible prosecution of Cathy Massiter.

British courts, after passing a sentence of imprisonment, as in the case of Harley Street's Dr Richards, sentenced to four years by an American court, do not afford trial judges the right to grant a defendant bail pending appeal – Dr Richards was even allowed to fly back to Britain to await his appeal! The American position seems to be more consistent with the presumption of innocence than the British one. Although British High Court judges have the right to grant bail pending appeal this is on the basis that they have to be persuaded that the panel has a real chance of success, i.e. they began upon the presumption that the conviction was well-founded. Not so the Americans who act on the basis that the liberty of the citizen should not be taken away until and unless every legal and constitutional avenue has been explored.

British courts do not allow for the doctrine of entrapment as exemplified by the acquittal of British car manufacturer John De Lorean recently in the Californian courts; indeed, even where it is shown that a crime in Britain was committed by police acting as agent provocateurs British law does not allow for acquittal on this ground.

British courts do not have anything remotely like the number of blacks, women and working-class persons as judges as the American courts. If one wants to see an effectively multiracial judiciary, with literally thousands of black judges, and women too in much profusion on the Bench, one avoids looking at Britain and looks to the United States.

(And one doubts whether any American judge, even the highest, or even the President of the United States even, could escape the censure and condemnation of his colleagues after making the remarks Lord Denning did. Senator Andrew Young was right when he said that Britain "practically invented racism!").

One of the most regrettable aspects of the British criminal courts is that defendants sit like caged animals in the dock while in the American courts attorney and client sit side by side – apart from making for quick and easy consultation this allows clear escape from the mantle of criminality which taints a defendant who sits in the dock guarded by prison warders. In British courts, even if a defendant is on bail a prison officer accompanies him to the witness box. American courts also have client, attorney and juries sitting on equal levels and, although there is dignity, there is not all the intimidating pomp and ceremony that make British courts almost a tourist attraction rather than a solemn business. Further, if physical inspection was made of the space allocation of the American courts it might be established that more space is reserved for the public ("the People") than in British courts.

Another matter of comparison between British and American courts is that British juries, after being discharged, are not allowed to discuss what prompted them to the conclusions they arrived at. But this is a pretence because every practising Barrister knows that jurors all over England discuss their views informally after trials; this is a great loss because if they were encouraged to discuss their views formally after the event, then research into trial by jury would be much assisted. And when British television wished to interview jurors about a case they would not have to travel to the USA, camera, microphones and all.

In Britain, the pretence about Sacred Juries is taken so far that newspapers like *The Observer* even write stories about barristers drinking with discharged jurors after a trial is over and yet the media and the Bar Council must know that jurors have drunk and will continue to drink with all and sundry all over the country. The danger is that pretence gives rise to guarded discussions and therefore the reservoir of research is denied. Not so in America where jurors are often interviewed in full view and hearing of press and public.

The above is not recorded merely mischievously but to advance the case for enlightened and well-informed jury research in England. It would be enlightening, for example, to discover what weight British juries attach to the clearly expressed "views" of the trial judge – if, upon enquiry, it was found that the "views" of the trial judge carry too much weight in the jury room then steps can be taken to inhibit the ability of the Judiciary to offer their own comment upon the evidence.

If, as further example, it is found upon enquiry that all-white juries find great difficulty in believing allegations made by blacks against the police then that might be cause and case for establishing black peoples' right to have at least six blacks on their jury.

If, in further example, it was found that Knightsbridge types believe the police every time against the defendant then that would be an argument for widening the catchment area of juries.

If it were found that former members of the armed forces always believed the police then, again, action could be taken. But action depends on research and research depends on accessibility and there can be no accessibility where the British legal system shrouds attitudes and reasoning of juries from the public.

When the question of abolishing trial by jury in fraud cases is raised it is a question of the blind leading the blind since nobody has bothered to ask the jurors, the very first persons to be asked!

The decision in the USA to charge "subway vigilante" Bernard Goetz with attempted murder gains added democratic strength because it comes from a U.S. Federal Grand Jury of citizens not, as in the U.K., where the D.P.P. alone can decide not to prosecute Brixton police officers who smashed up black people's homes on the Frontline as acts of revenge for their humiliation in the Brixton riots. One can imagine that a similar Grand Jury system here could well decimate the ranks of those policemen who sometimes take the law, and blazing guns, into their own hands.

The net effect of the exclusion of the blacks and the Irish and working-classes from the high offices of the legal profession is to increase the polarisation between an establishment-oriented profession and those excluded from it, and more and more blacks and minority groups are asking why they cannot see their own kind represented on the Bench. Isolation of any section of the community cannot be good for society and I personally cannot begin to believe that I will see black High Court judges and black MPs this side of the twenty-first century.

A society that continues to deny equality for its minorities while unemployment queues lengthen is a society that is storing up trouble for itself and, as black youths take more and more to the streets (and as blacks learn more and more to equate their position with the Freedom Fighters of Northern Ireland against the British Army of Occupation), while the British police are training and arming more and more for confrontation in the streets, while prolific use of firearms becomes more and more the accepted norm in British society, one cannot help but feel that the Falklands conquest, including the disgraceful sinking of the Belgrano, has sharpened British memory of Empire and British thirst for military solutions to political problems; the martyrdom of miners' leader Arthur Scargill for defiance of the courts is inevitable because the miners know what advocates of "black sections" in the Labour Party do not realise – both miners' shackles and black political isolation are founded, nay anchored, in the roots of militarism and colonialism (the miners would say capitalism) and such interests of domination and exploitation cannot be reasoned with to give up their spoils – only acts of radical militancy can claw back any semblance of equality within the current structure of British society. Slavery and Empire were born of the same instincts as the Falklands "war" and the exploitation of the Catholics in Northern Ireland and the lessons of history cannot be denied.

A propos the miners' strike one has only to add together the cost of the subsidy of the Falklands Garrison, the cost of keeping British troops in Northern Ireland, the cost of Polaris, Trident and other exotic missiles to see that the question of "subsidising" what Mrs Thatcher calls "uneconomic mines" is a mockery of the sweat, toil and tears of generations of miners and their families whose bones literally litter the mines of South Wales and other well-known mining areas.

Leaving aside the relatively minor question as to whether the amount paid out in dole money would in any event exceed the total collective subsidy of keeping mines open and miners employed, the question of "uneconomic mines" is linked also to the question of heavy investment in modern machinery by a Government almost wholly obsessed with conflict abroad and confrontation with the workers at home.

We hear nothing but condemnation of violence on the picket lines but who condemns the violence and the havoc wrought on the self-respect not to mention the shopping bags of miners and their wives – are whole communities to be wiped out while millions are wasted daily on garrisons abroad and preparation for nuclear war at home? The Labour Party and the Alliance must resist the temptation to trim their sails after each electoral storm and must set their course clearly –either nuclear weapons (and the macabre possibility of nuclear war) are desirable or they are not; if not then they must support Joan Ruddock's legendary CND with total passion and absolute will. Either they support the miners' struggle wholeheartedly or not at all – the present social upheaval over this question can only be resolved by devotion to total radicalism and not opportunistic trimming of sails.

And one wonders why, for example, Ken Livingstone (whatever his faults, perhaps one of the greatest democrats of British politics currently), should now be labelled and hunted down as "anti-semitic" at a time when his is the loudest voice for the rights of minorities. The instinct for class and race control includes the international politics of domination by Zionism and all those who argue for a better society, from Jesse Jackson and Andrew Young in the USA, to Yasser Arafat in the Middle East to Ken Livingstone in London, understand too well that the politics of international Zionism include the politics of the denial of equality of the working-classes, including the blacks and the Irish in Great Britain and the Palestinians in the Middle East. The shooting of C.B.S. cameramen by Israelis in Lebanon is very much the style of Zionism.

What resort therefore do those "left out" of control of the machinery of State have? Ask the Catholics in Northern Ireland and the Palestinians in the Middle East! But I might weakly state that those who appear for the citizen client in the Criminal courts are the best hope yet for the citizen faced with a battle against police and, sometimes, some few members of the judiciary. And, to this limited effect, Barristers for the Defence offer some slight, temporary hope to the recipients of oppression.

While considering the denial of "black sections" by Neil Kinnock and the Labour Party, black radicals should record that the more subtle and sophisticated Jewish community have themselves set up "Jewish sections" by silently and secretly noting that they must support the coming of Jewish MPs and they work to this end with feverish and overpowering zeal – blacks still believe in open and honest politics; well, brothers and sisters, they can see you coming miles away and only united determination within black organisations with the power to demand seats and deliver votes Jesse Jackson style will secure black Parliamentary representation this side of the 21st century.

In this context it is revealing to watch the machinations and manoeuvres of the British Labour Party as the party hierarchy sets out to re-nominate Sidney Bidwell for the Southall constituency while finding procedural fault with the Asian Councillors who have sweated for years to return the Asian vote to Labour. Side by side with the Southall saga, one watches with interest to see whether black Councillor Diane Abbott will get the Brent East nomination or whether Labour's left in Brent, as I predict, will prefer to hand the safe seat over to a white "kith-and-kin" candidate from outside Brent. Paul Boateng, probably the best hope for our second black MP this century (if half-Jewish Paul is black then half-Pakistani Tory MP Jonathan Sayeed must already demonstrate that the Tories have led the way, not Labour!), may well watch the safe Brent South seat slip away as Labour's white votes defect, as did David Pitt's fifteen years ago in Clapham! And watch Roger Scrutton's article in *The Times* on 5th March, 1985, when he points out that the natural political party of the Asian community should be the Tory Party; if philosophy and practice is anything to go by, the Labour Party should be deserted in droves by Britain's blacks, if only as an act of retribution for Labour's continuing treachery.

A propos the denial of "black sections" in the Labour Party, it is worth stating in this book of records that some of the same "honourable" members of Neil Kinnock's Labour Party who oppose "black sections" were equally in hand with the Tories when the Zimbabwean constitution was amended to enshrine the necessity of "white MPs" in Zimbabwe! This hypocrisy and betrayal by the Labour Party of black and Irish and minority interests should really entitle them to one great, political kick in their treacherous backsides at the next General Election!

But there is more, much more for the Defence Barrister to know and debate about and one of these things is the Police and Criminal Evidence Act, 1984.

Variously described as the only answer to rising crime and as a devastating blow to civil liberties, there is no doubt that the final Act offers plenteous food for thought for the aspiring criminal practitioner. One of the new powers conferred on Thatcherite Britain's police is the power of senior officers to block roads military-style for up to seven days on suspicion of serious arrestable offence – very much in the military tradition of the occupation forces of Northern Ireland. Solicitors and family may be barred for up to 36 hours and one immediately asks the question: "Why?"

Doctors may search mouth, anus and vagina for drugs and weapons and so may police officers search mouth, anus and vagina for "weapons"! The British Medical Association say that such searches by doctors without consent is unethical but the police are not so ethically bound. Fingerprints, photographs and body samples will be taken with or without consent so that the human body is no longer inviolate once it finds itself inside a police station. Mind you, they've been doing this to Irish women detainees for years and nobody has really protested!

There is no power to search the homes of third parties for evidence so God help the ordinary man if one of his friends is arrested. And, in this democracy of democracies, unlawfully or improperly obtained evidence may be admitted unless the trial judge thinks it would unfairly influence the trial – so may previous convictions! "Where oh where" is the presumption of innocence and all the rules of evidence as to material illegally obtained! Even involuntary confessions may be obtained "if the judge thinks they are reliable."

All the above, of course, makes a mockery of the rules of the presumption of innocence and it is clear that Britain's Police now have a Charter – a Licence – to run riot through our streets and homes if they wish. This Act is the most obscene bit of legislation ever to come on to the Statute Books of England and should be resisted by all lawful means possible.

Jointly for consideration with the above is the Newman Method of Infiltration of organisations, particularly black ones, by officers of the Involvement Units of the Metropolitan Police. Wherever one looks in London, more and more minority organisations, and "community relations" ones too, are sporting more and more police officers among their guests at meetings and other functions. The West Indian Ex-Servicemen's Association has led the field in that its Chairman is a presently-serving police officer! Defence Barristers now have to be aware and wary of this infiltration because police officers only infiltrate if it is Force Policy to do so and their promotion prospects are much enhanced. The result is that a lot more secret files are being built up on the black and minority leadership so that subtle police blackmail/persuasion becomes more effective.

This political self-castration by some of Britain's minority organisa-tions has gone too far.

Eyes by now should be blinded by the red lights but the police brainwash their victims to resist criticism and castrate in turn their chief critics. It is therefore no wonder that the quality of debate injected into meetings of the famed Lambeth Police Consultative Committee by some of Lambeth's minority "leadership" is spineless and innocuous – police have files on some of them and, in regard to others, massive physical and psychological strangulation; so that one hears the occasional whine but no one speaks out boldly against police misconduct. Thus it was possible for the DPP to refuse to prosecute police officers who smashed down doors and television sets on Brixton's post-riot Frontline with axes and sledgehammers without raising a great howl of public protest and it is even possible for police representatives, while asserting *sub judice* rules to stifle debate on allegations of police misconduct, nevertheless to give their own version of controversial events – the playing down of the allegedly brutal attack on reggae singer Junior Service was a noted instance of successful police domination and dominance of this Committee. One does not blame the police – one congratulates them; but one does lose sleep over some of the so-called community "leadership" cheerfully kept in tow by a now over-politicised police force. The effect is to stultify at source and at nearly every meeting any hope for open debate on policing because the police always take the initiative and the others follow – as a Public Relations springboard for the police it takes some beating – the danger is that it pretends to be other than that which it really is – a vehicle for police propaganda. Defence Barristers charged with the defence of a man arrested in controversial circumstances may find their guns well and truly spiked in advance by the police having already addressed the reservoir of South London Press-reading jurors with their version of events. But it must not be thought that police zeal and planning is limited to the specific and the particular. What we are witnessing, although some cannot or refuse to see it, is a massive propaganda and credibility build-up by the Metropolitan Police so that jurors begin to take less and less easily allegations of police misconduct – it is a smokescreen to blind the eyes and deceive the hearts and minds of jurors well in advance of public trial. Not only public trial, the rash police action (in March) in the seige of Philbeach Gardens, London, earned only muted media protest.

The Lambeth Police Liaison Committee's deliberations merely prove that the Police and the non-Police Committee members get on well together – it does *not* prove that Officer X did not brutalise Mr Y or Officer A did not tell lies against Mr B – taken hand in hand with the draconian powers of the new Police Act (1984) the powers of policing have now taken on a political edge of infiltration and subtle intimidation of public stances of so-called responsible leaders.

It might be argued that the black/Irish/gay minority communities are more and more being riddled with police informers and that the police will get their secret files anyway – this, however, is not the point. The point is that minority organisations, in the presence of a large number of police officers, cannot engage in free and true debate on police issues – their conclusions, when debated and voted on in the presence of police officers, therefore tend to follow false and servile courses and lack the hard, intellectual integrity of debate among non-police members, informers or no informers. The revelations of Clive Ponting and Cathy Massiter, re MI5 and secret files, is the very context of this argument.

We are not of course advocating that police officers should never be invited to speak to or meet with community groups. (I have always advocated dialogue and even cricket or social meetings.)

West Indian Standing Conference's Director William Trant has never failed to invite top police officers to meet with and discuss policing with Conference but police officers have never been allowed to dominate Conference thinking or embarrass Conference debates as with, unhappily, certain other black organisations.

Indeed, Paul Boateng's advocacy of "police accountability" to those who pay them and employ them has been turned on its head by Commissioner Newman's Involvement Units in that these Involvement Units, by their penetration and depth of association and social engagement and by subtle intimidation methods mentioned above, have made certain black organisations accountable to the police – not quite what the eloquent Paul Boateng intended or advocates!

There is a clear and abiding determination at New Scotland Yard that London must be held in the stranglehold of a wide and thorough police political and social network and this stranglehold effectively stifles clear perception of police conduct and suffocates free ability to voice open criticism – what is heard is a strangled cry before the potential shouter is ostracised and discredited.

Nothing in the above is meant to detract from the integrity, industry and expertise of 'L' Division's Commander Alex Marnock who, with his officers, has brought a new sensitivity and openness to policing. He answers to the compliment of a 'canny Scot' but his geniality hides an ability to be tough and firm without being discourteous or malicious – the only thing he lacks is good, hard, articulate Guyanese opposition!

Side-by-side with the above is the entrenched ability of the media to disregard allegations against the police and to concentrate only on the sensationalism that attends convictions of blacks and minorities in the criminal courts.

On the 13th November, 1984, at the Birmingham Crown Court, two men, George Tomkins and Lionel Webb, were acquitted of serious charges after accusing the West Midlands Crime Squad of perjury and frame-up. The media, including the "enlightened" *Observer* newspaper, chose to ignore all the allegations of police misconduct and concentrated frivolously instead on post-acquittal "drinking sessions" between jurors and lawyers – they even chose to ignore the presence of police officers and journalists at the "drinking sessions!" Their treatment of the matter was so as to invite public inference that the acquittals may well have been secured by unorthodox methods!

Barristers for the Defence need to be aware of the parallel and incestuous pressures wielded jointly and in unison by police, media and some members of the legal profession.

The above may well be seen as one man's myopic and prejudiced view of certain current and contemporaneous topics in British society but this is exactly what trial by jury is all about – when addressing twelve good men and true one is addressing the twelve individual and collective prejudices of twelve lifetimes and while everyone keeps urging a jury to act only on the evidence the ability of a jury to allow for, say, brutality by police officers is tailored by their own education, formal and informal, so that, for example, a Knightsbridge jury, well-tailored and well-heeled, shopping at Harrods and slumming it at Ascot, finds such allegations clearly out of their perception because such matters are clearly out of their personal experience while a Snaresbrook Crown Court has no psychological difficulty at all in believing in police arrogance and contempt of East Enders. Attitudes, prejudices, biases – that's what trial by jury is all about and that is why Brixton Barristers will always beat hell out of Cambridge-types!

It must be remarked that Britain, and the British Parliament, is fundamentally, inherently and almost irretrievably class-ridden and racist – when you stand up to defend a Rasta or an Irishman or a Cockney then you could have a tough job on your hands – Defence work in the Criminal Courts is no picnic!

At the end of the Longest Day, a Barrister for the Defence must realise that he is the only and final filter between citizen, client and the State and he must brook no interference, tolerate no impertinence or incompetence, suffer all hardships and even be prosecuted by the Bar Council for speaking his mind. Better be prosecuted for speaking the Truth than for telling lies!

To be a Barrister for the Defence without peer is be very much The Outsider leading sometimes to a life of loneliness and ostracism. But all pioneers suffer this fate – as Marcus Garvey said: "Leadership means many things: Pain, Suffering – even Death" and the role of the honest, committed Barrister for the Defence very often invites attack from all those who wilt at the fundamental right of the citizen to a vigorous Defence Counsel. To this end therefore potential leading Barristers for the Defence would do well to study not only law but the lessons of History, Colonialism, even Genocide – they are the Frontline Fighters and will receive Frontline attention from hostile sections – but, if your Powder is Dry and your Hands Steady – then: "Pass the Ammunition, Brother, I am going over that Hill!"